WARNING

This book is not for women.

Nor is it for softies, wimps or nerds who intend to stay that way for the rest of their lives.

It is not for Christians who think they've got it made, who already know what following Christ is all about, or who are in any other way completely saved.

Nor is it for he-men, rugged individualists or self-made men who have their act together and who see no need to change.

This book is for men who know they aren't perfect and are willing to admit it. It is for men who sense a need for self-development but who are not quite sure of what needs to be developed. It is for men who feel a desire for personal growth and who are willing to listen to some suggestions. It is for Christians who have heard a call for a deeper conversion in their lives but don't know what to make of it.

It is a book about the human spirit, and in particular, about the masculine spirit in every human being. It is a book about male energy, about tapping into it and about running with it. It is a book about developing the spiritual potential to change oneself and, in doing so, to change the world.

If you are not up to that, or if you don't want to do that, close this book immediately. This book is not for you.

On the other hand, if you are willing to be challenged, if you are open to being changed, strengthened and deepened, read on—even if you are a woman, but especially if you want to be a man.

Richard Rohr and Joseph Martos

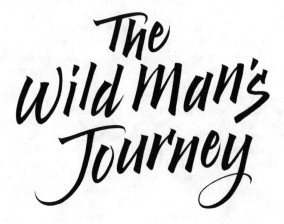

The Wild Man's Journey

REFLECTIONS ON MALE SPIRITUALITY

ST.
ANTHONY
MESSENGER
PRESS

CINCINNATI, OHIO

Nihil Obstat: Rev. Robert L. Hagedorn
Rev. Nicholas Lohkamp, O.F.M.

Imprimi Potest: Rev. John Bok, O.F.M.
Provincial

Imprimatur: +James H. Garland, V.G.
Archdiocese of Cincinnati
December 3, 1991

The *nihil obstat* and *imprimatur* are a declaration that a book is considered to be free from doctrinal or moral error. It is not implied that those who have granted the *nihil obstat* and *imprimatur* agree with the contents, opinions or statements expressed.

Cover and book design by Julie Lonneman.

Jacket illustration by John Quigley, O.F.M.

Calligraphy by Patti Paulus.

ISBN 0-86716-128-0

Published by St. Anthony Messenger Press
Printed in the U.S.A.

"A man, yet by these tears a little boy again,
Throwing myself on the sand, confronting the waves,
I, chanter of pains and joys, uniter of here and hereafter,
Taking all hints to use them, but swiftly leaping beyond them,
A reminiscence sing."
                         —Walt Whitman, "Out of the Cradle Endlessly Rocking"

Foreword

When St. Anthony Messenger Press asked me to collaborate with Richard Rohr on a book about male spirituality as a follow-up to our other books (*The Great Themes of Scripture: Old Testament*, 1987; *The Great Themes of Scripture: New Testament*, 1988; and *Why Be Catholic? Understanding Our Experience and Tradition*, 1989), I immediately began to read everything I could on the subject. There wasn't much to read because there wasn't much written about male spirituality.

I found only four books, all written rather recently, that even broached the topic: *What Men Are Like* by John Sanford and George Lough (Paulist, 1988); *The Intimate Connection* by James Nelson (Westminster, 1988); *A Man and His God* by Martin W. Pable (Ave Maria, 1988); and *Toward a Male Spirituality* by John Carmody (Twenty-Third, 1989). Of these four, only one—the book by Father Pable (who, like Richard, is a Franciscan and a retreat director)—even came close to what Richard had to say about men and their spiritual development. I knew then that what Richard was saying was new and important, and that it should be put into print. So I agreed to go ahead with the project.

This book was based initially on four talks that Richard gave as a weekend retreat for men only. Women were not invited because the retreat intended to bring up issues of primary concern to men and because portions of the weekend were set aside for small-group sessions in which men could process concerns that they might not raise in the presence of women. The intention was to create an atmosphere in which suppressed doubts and fears, hopes and dreams could safely come to the surface, be listened to and be discussed in frank, man-to-man dialogue.

Those who read this book may want to use the ideas presented in a similar fashion, either by themselves, in a small group of other men or even with female partners. To facilitate this somewhat meditative use of the material, I divided Richard's comments into sections, each of which focuses on one main idea. Some sections are longer and some are shorter, but readers familiar with the audiocassette tapes which first presented most of this material will find that the flow of topics is similar to the original retreat.

The audiocassette program from which the book was developed is *A Man's Approach to God*, published by St. Anthony Messenger Press (1984). Before setting to work on the project, however, Richard asked if I could incorporate some new material from a more recent program, *The Spirit in a Man*, published by Credence Cassettes (1988).

Initially in this collaboration, I wanted to deliberately stick close to Richard's own words, but as Richard knows by now, I wasn't able to be as faithful to that intention as

I tried to be. Fortunately for me, Richard is a very understanding coauthor, and he assures me that despite the changes in the wording (his speaking style is very different from my writing style), he can see his ideas coming through words that are often my own.

Nevertheless, because Richard feels strongly about this subject, he wanted to include some thoughts in his own words. These thoughts will be found in Chapters Six, Seven, Twenty-one and Twenty-eight, as well as in the Afterword. The result, I trust, is a harmony of two different voices.

Joseph Martos

Contents

The Task of Integration

All growth is difficult and painful. My own insights into
the process and my answers to the questions that people
ask me inevitably come out of my own experience, as
well as from my reading and talking with others. You
may find some of the books that will be cited in the
footnotes more helpful than what I am about to say here,
which is one reason they are mentioned in this book.
The experiences and insights of other authors may be
closer to what you need to hear, as you go on to take the
next step in your spiritual development.

My own insights into the spiritual growth needs of
men come largely out of my experiences in two very
different pastoring situations. For a little more than
thirteen years I was the pastor of New Jerusalem in
Cincinnati, Ohio, which can best be described as an
intentional community. New Jerusalem was founded by
myself and others with the intention of creating a
Christian community which was deliberately different
from the usual Catholic models of the local parish and
the religious order. For the past few years, however, I
have been a codirector of the Center for Action and

Contemplation in Albuquerque, New Mexico. Instead of trying to create a community as such, those of us at the center are ministering to others who are working for social justice and nonviolent change. Already a fine network has emerged among us, but this community has come about as a by-product of our action-oriented yet contemplative ministry. Both situations require and foster spiritual growth, but in different ways.

My experience in New Jerusalem taught me much about the need for men to develop their feminine side, as well as about ways to go about actually doing this. I was twenty-eight when the community was founded, and most of the young men during those early years were in their late teens to early thirties. As a group, the spiritual task confronting us was to move from the common masculine and into the feminine side of our nature. The presence of women and, eventually, children in the community encouraged us to develop the feminine virtues of listening, empathy, dialogue and trust that are so needed for community, both within the family and in the larger social group. Many in the community, both men and women, developed their interpersonal skills to an extraordinary degree, and the community as a whole grew in its wisdom about relationships and the dynamics of living together. Visitors marveled at our ability to get in touch with what was going on inside ourselves and in one another, and to process all of that in coming to make community decisions. That sensitivity and practical wisdom is still one of the great strengths of New Jerusalem.

In the late 1970's, though, something began to happen which unsettled this feminine emphasis on relationship and community. I gave my first retreats to priests in the Third World at that time, but I was probably changed more by what I saw and heard outside America than the priests were affected by anything I said to them. When I returned to New Jerusalem to share what I had witnessed of political and economic oppression, many in the community seemed unwilling or unable to respond to it in any positive way.

Looking back, I might call what happened then a crisis of the subjective versus the objective. We in the community had become masters of the subjective and relational, the interpersonal and the familial, but as a group we had no skill and little desire to deal with objective situations outside our own. We could talk endlessly about how we felt, but we did not know how to cope with objective situations where what we felt did not matter in the least. These were situations that cried out for action, not for feeling.

When I challenged New Jerusalem to take an active interest in the redemption of society, many resisted by charging that I was attempting to change the definition and direction of their community. Interestingly, the loudest voices in this group were often men. They had found in New Jerusalem a vibrant and alive space where, for the first time in their lives, they could develop their deprived femininity, and they felt threatened by the possibility of losing that privileged experience. Some people even left the community because of what they heard me preaching about America's exploitation of the Third World and the need to work for social justice. Again, most of these were men, because these men had a lot more to question about their jobs, their life-styles and their political allegiances than did the women.

The women, it seemed, were a great deal freer to hear what I was saying and to begin to act on it. Part of that may have been because they were more sensitive to the needs of others, and part of it may have been because they were not controlled by careers based on competition and consumption. Much of the women's ability to move in a new direction, though, was due to the fact that they were ready to move into their masculine side, much more than the men were ready to move out of their newly discovered femininity.

Eventually, however, New Jerusalem weathered the crisis and developed an orientation toward redemptive action in addition to its initial orientation toward community building. During the time that I was the pastor, there were differences of opinion, but there was no total split in the community between those who favored working on relationship and family needs and those who preferred working on peace and justice issues. Perhaps that's because as the founder, so to speak, I was able to provide the community with a father figure whom everyone could either fight or follow.

Since the time I left New Jerusalem to begin a new ministry in 1986, I am told that people in the community often settle into one of two camps. Those who feel a continuing need to develop the feminine are working rather constantly in the area of the subjective, and those who feel the need to develop the masculine are working more and more in the area of objective action. The two groups still respect one another, but there is not as much integration of the two orientations as either would hope for. I believe that this is something of a loss in the life of the community, but perhaps it is one of the inevitable pains of growth—that we do not all grow at the same rate or in the same direction all at once.

If in New Jerusalem we were trying to integrate the masculine with the feminine, you could say that those of us at the Center for Action and Contemplation are trying to integrate the feminine with the masculine. We are aiming at the same goal, but we are approaching it from the opposite direction. As its name suggests, the center is geared toward action, which is on the masculine side of spirituality, but it is also a place for contemplation, which is on the feminine side.

Except for the center's relatively small staff, we do not envision building community as much as we do building ministers. Those who come to us on internships are either preparing for the ministry of peace and justice or are already active in it. They come to be empowered or to be rejuvenated for a work to which they are already committed. We make available to them everything from spiritual direction to professional massages if they need it, we offer them active training in local work among the poor and we supply a network of contacts that can support them when they return to their respective ministries. Perhaps most importantly, we provide a space where they can gather with other ministers to reflect on their work, receive encouragement from others who are doing what they are doing and gain insight into working more effectively.

As you can tell, the center has a bias toward action, and that's deliberate. One of the best-selling books of the 1980's was *In Search of Excellence*, in which the authors analyzed the most successful businesses in America.[1] They found that without exception the most dynamic companies were those that had a bias toward action. Instead of endlessly planning and reconsidering, submitting ideas through committee after committee and generating mountains of paperwork, the successful businesses were those geared to taking new ideas and running with them. By putting the ideas into action first, they were able to test the ideas against reality to see which ones produced and which ones had to be discarded or revised. In contrast, the companies that theorized first and refined ideas in the abstract before putting them into practice were just as likely to have to change their approach afterwards—but by then they had lost the advantage of initial action.

Believe it or not, this same contrast between the bias toward reflection and the bias toward action has a counterpart in traditional Catholic spirituality. The bias toward reflection is epitomized in the approach of Ignatius of Loyola, or Jesuit spirituality, and the bias toward action is exemplified in the approach of Francis of Assisi or Franciscan spirituality.

The Jesuit approach to discerning what to do when a decision is called for is prayerful, theoretical and reflective. You take time out and think about the decision and the various alternatives, talking them over with a spiritual director who helps you to understand the possible implications of the different options, the teachings of the Scriptures or the doctrines of the Church that might illuminate your decision, and your

---

[1]Peters, Thomas J., and Robert H. Waterman. *In Search of Excellence: Lessons from America's Best Run Companies.* New York, N.Y.: Harper and Row, 1982.

own conscious or unconscious motivations in the whole matter. If the decision is a big one, it is preferable that you go on a thirty-day retreat to pray, think and sort things out before making your decision. It is a sound approach to decisionmaking, but not everyone has the luxury to take so much time out for discernment.

The Franciscan method of discernment is just the opposite. St. Francis had a habit of asking what God wanted him to do, taking the Scriptures at their word and then doing it. In modern terms we might say that Francis had a habit of radical and even simplistic obedience to the Scriptures, but however we might name it, it was a bias toward action. Sometimes he would find a passage in the Gospel and he'd simply do it, figuring that if he was misinterpreting God's will, his decision wouldn't work out. Instead of trying to work it all out in his head first, he let action be his teacher. For Francis, reflection was something to do after, not before, acting. When he didn't have inner certitude as to which road he should take, he would literally stand at the crossroads, twirl around and go in the direction he landed. The will of God for Francis was simply the willingness to *do* the will of God.

In a Church as large and diverse as ours, there is certainly room for both types of discernment and both are probably preferable at different times. (And it is good if we stretch ourselves to our less preferred style once in a while.) Both are ways of understanding God's will and doing it, and of combining feminine receptiveness and masculine assertiveness. In our affluent society, where we have the leisure to think things out, we naturally prefer the Jesuit style of discernment. In the Third

World, however, liberation theologians point out what our own Supreme Court stated with reference to racial segregation, that justice delayed is justice denied. When waiting to decide means that more children will die of malnutrition, that more people will die of infectious diseases, that more individuals will be killed by death squads, that more Church workers will be abducted, that more farmers will be pushed from their land, that more families will be destroyed and that more people will be condemned to live in poverty and squalor, then failing to act means failing to be a Christian. This is why liberation theology insists on the importance of *praxis*—applying the gospel in a practical way to the problems of society.

The gospel of Jesus is not a theory for reflection but a plan of action. Jesus does not tell us what to think so much as he tells us what to do. He tells us to love God above all and to love our neighbor as well. He tells us to work for justice and to risk persecution for it. He tells us to give to the poor, to visit the imprisoned, to comfort the afflicted, to clothe the naked and to shelter the homeless. He even makes it a command: "This is my commandment: love one another as I love you" (John 15:12). The way that Jesus loved was to lay down his life for others.

Most of the teaching of Jesus is really rather clear and needs no heavy discernment as to *whether*; the only discernment might be *how* or *when*. We are finally ready to hear Jesus when we recognize that problems of injustice are not solved by soft charity or spiritualization. Following Jesus means following in his footsteps. The only choice we have is to follow or not, to be a disciple or not, to be a Christian or not, even though none of us will do it perfectly.

Living in this material world, with a physical body, and in a culture of affluence which rewards the outer self, it is both more difficult and all the more necessary to know our spiritual center.

How do you find what is supposedly already there? Why isn't it obvious? How do you awaken the center? By thinking about it? By praying and meditating? By more silence and solitude? Yes, perhaps, but mostly by *living*—and living consciously. The edges suffered and enjoyed lead us back to the center. The street person feels cold and rejection and has to go to a deeper place for warmth. The hero pushes against his own self-interested edges and finds that they don't matter. The alcoholic man recognizes how he has hurt his family and breaks through to a compassion beyond himself.

In each case the edges suffer, inform, partially self-destruct, and all are found to be unnecessary and even part of the problem. That which feels the pain also lets it go and the center stands revealed and sufficient! We do not find our own center; it finds us. The body is in the soul. It is both the place of contact and the place of surrender. We don't think ourselves into a new way of living. We live ourselves into a new way of thinking. The journeys around the circumference lead us to life at the center.

Then by what is certainly a vicious and virtuous circle, the center calls all the journeys at the circumference into question! The ruthless ambition of the businessman can lead him to the very failure and emptiness that is the point of his conversion. Is the ambition, therefore, good or evil? Do we really have to sin to know salvation? Call me a "sin mystic," but that is exactly what I see happening in *all* my pastoral experience.

That does not mean that we should set out to intentionally sin. We only see the pattern after the fact. Julian of Norwich put it perfectly, "Commonly, first we fall and later we see it—and both are the Mercy of God." Wow! How did we ever lose that? It got hidden away in that least celebrated but absolutely central Easter Vigil Service when the deacon sings to the Church about a "felix culpa," the happy fault which precedes and necessitates the eternal Christ.

If Christ is the perfect archetype of the eternal man, and I think he is, then our path is somehow the same as his: to move from top to bottom, from fullness to emptiness, from mere word to planetary flesh. It is called Incarnation and it is another name for salvation. That is the style and the hope of this book.

>>> 2 <<<

Male and Female God Created Them

I once saw a painting in the Grace Episcopal Cathedral in San Francisco which symbolically represents masculinity and femininity as they are experienced in our culture. One could even call this painting mythic as well as symbolic because it expresses in an image what we feel about ourselves as men and as women at a very deep level. Perhaps that is why the painting was hung in the rear of the cathedral—because it touches something deep in the human soul, it arrests one's attention and it calls forth contemplation.

The painting shows six figures, three male and three female, interwoven in a circle. The description next to the painting calls the three male figures the Lords, and it gives them the names Mind, Form and Speech. These three look outward from the circle, symbolically observing, defining and naming reality. Their energy is directed away from themselves in three separate directions. The female figures are called the Muses, and they are named Meditation, Memory and Song. These three look toward one another, symbolically beholding, recalling and affirming relationship. Their energy moves toward the center of the circle, toward togetherness and unity.

There is a beautiful symmetry in this artistic portrayal of the masculine and the feminine in our lives. Not only does it symbolize how we often feel about ourselves as men and as women, it also expresses how we experience the masculine and feminine dimensions within ourselves. It reminds me that in the Bible humanity is created male and female in God's image (Genesis 1:27) and that the distinction between man and woman is placed after their original unity (Genesis 2:18-23).

For countless ages, however, human culture and society have emphasized the differences between men and women rather than their underlying unity. Despite the endless fascination of the sexes for one another, social customs have sharply distinguished maleness from femaleness and sexual morality has been concerned with keeping men and women apart. Our society has taught us to regard the opposite sex with suspicion, and our culture has bred in us a spirit of competition for different forms of power.

Since most cultures have been patriarchal or dominated by men, women are usually viewed—especially by those in the feminist movement—as an oppressed group in society. The general assumption is that men have all the power and that women are the losers. In my own reflections on the male-female antagonism, however, I have come to see that both men and women are the losers. We are deprived of that healthy wholeness—and, I would even say, holiness—which comes from integrating both the masculine and the feminine in our lives as men or women. I would even go so far as to suggest that by and large men suffer greater deprivation than women. They also suffer more as a result of this deprivation.

What I mean by this is that women can often compensate for the cultural stereotype in which they have been cast by engaging in the masculine power game. True, they have usually had to do this in the past in stereotypically feminine ways, subtly and indirectly employing their womanly wiles to manipulate the men around them. Men, however, have not had a similar avenue open to them. Female behavior was so strictly taboo that men have been blocked from recognizing and developing the feminine dimension within them, the feminine side of being wholly human.

In recent years theologians in the Third World have made it very clear that much of the gospel proclaimed by Jesus and lived by the early Church was concerned with human liberation. The "good news" (which is the root meaning of the word gospel) is that people can be freed from the oppression that binds them. The good news is that those who accept God's love can live in God's kingdom and not be trapped in the world. The good news is that those who care for one another the way that Jesus did can begin to live in the kingdom of heaven right now because they are freed from the entanglements that make life hell. Life can be a nightmare for women and men, slaves and masters, poor and rich alike until they are liberated by God's love put into practice.

The first to accept and respond to the gospel message of liberation were, of course, the poor and the powerless. They were blessed because they knew that they were poor and in need of salvation (Matthew 5:3-12). Much of Jesus' teaching, however, was directed not at the poor but at the rich, not at the weak but at the powerful. Jesus evidently saw the oppressors (often typified in the first three Gospels as "the scribes and the Pharisees") as needing salvation as much as the oppressed. If anything, their need for liberation was even greater because they were trapped by their own blindness (Matthew 23:13-39).

What Jesus saw so clearly in his own day is still true today. The rich are deprived by their own wealth, the powerful are victimized by their own positions, the oppressors are oppressed by their own authoritarian behavior. They may not see it this way, but it is nonetheless true.

Applying this gospel lesson to the male-female antagonism, we have to conclude that men, the supposedly dominant group, are in as great or greater need of salvation when compared with women. They think they have power, but they are mostly powerless. They think they have freedom, but they are largely unliberated. They think they are the Lords, defining reality, but in fact they are trapped—trapped at the top.

If this is the case, then women have nothing to gain by turning the situation upside down. Some feminists seem to believe that if the male-female roles could be reversed, women would be liberated from oppression in our patriarchal society. If the roles were simply reversed, however, women would become just as trapped as men now are, but in a matriarchal or woman-dominated system.

The liberating gospel of Jesus is that salvation is

found not in domination but in partnership, not in power-wielding but in power-sharing. The poor are not saved by robbing the rich. The weak are not saved by conquering the strong. The oppressed are not saved by making the masters their slaves. Turning the tables simply perpetuates the sinful human situation that Jesus was engaged in redeeming.

The gospel message that liberation comes through the sharing of power has many implications for society such as the need for community, cooperation and communication between otherwise opposed social groups. Liberation theologians have articulated the need for wealth-sharing between the First and Third Worlds, for resource-sharing between developed and underdeveloped countries and for political power-sharing between majority and minority ethnic groups. Only if gifts are shared will the world begin to experience the gospel reality of the Kingdom of God.

The implication of this good news for personal spirituality is analogous to this. The masculine spirit, the male dimension of our soul, has gifts which can be characterized, as they are in the cathedral painting, as Mind, Form and Speech. They are the left-brain powers of logic and language, clarity and distinctness, thinking and deciding, organization and order. I call it the "art of separation." The feminine spirit, on the other hand, has gifts which can be characterized as Meditation, Memory and Song. These are the right-brain powers of creativity and intuition, comprehension and synthesis, feeling and affectivity, relationship and connection. I call these the "art of union."

Separation without union is only alienation and

loneliness. Union without separation is addiction and co-dependency. In either case there is no love, which is what spirituality is always about.

The spiritually whole person integrates within himself or herself both the masculine and the feminine dimensions of the human spirit. She or he is androgynous in the best sense of that term, which is derived from the two Greek words meaning "man" and "woman." Neither side dominates because each energizes the other, and each is empowered by the other. Androgyny is the ability to be masculine in a womanly way and to be feminine in a manly way. The androgynous person distinguishes the masculine from the feminine, which is the male gift, but also unites the masculine and the feminine, which is the female gift. Androgyny is the capacity of the spiritually whole person to be both male and female and to use the energies from both in a decisive yet creative manner.[2]

The painting of the Lords and the Muses is a marvelous symbol of androgyny precisely because it distinguishes the masculine from the feminine while uniting them in a single work of art. At first it presents us with the surface myths of the male and the female, but after continued viewing it invites us to look beyond the separate stereotypes and comprehend them within an integrated whole. Perhaps that is why the artist, Peter Rogers, entitled his work "The New Paradigm." He was trying to present a new image of what it means to be human: neither exclusively male nor exclusively female but a balanced interplay of both.

---

[2]For more on androgyny, read *The Invisible Partners*, by John A. Sanford (Paulist Press, 1980).

Such is the vision we must achieve if we are even to think about spirituality today. And such is the goal we must keep before us if we are ever to attain that holiness which is wholeness.

>>> **3** <<<

The White Male System

"In a world of fugitives,
the person taking the opposite direction
will appear to run away."
—T. S. Eliot, *The Family Reunion*[3]

Anne Wilson Schaef is a psychologist who in recent
years has written a number of books about addiction and
codependence, caused not only by drugs but also by the
way people think and behave in modern society.[4] When
she first began writing about the social system that we in
America live and work in, she labeled it the white male
system because our culture is dominated by white
males. Afterwards, however, she came to the realization
that many women have also bought into this system and
that they defend it just as strenuously as most men do.
She also saw that this is but one of a number of systems

---

[3]Eliot, T. S. *The Family Reunion.* New York, N.Y.: Harcourt, Brace Jovanovich
Publishers, 1939, p. 110.
[4]Her works include *Women's Reality: An Emerging Female System in the White
Male Society* (Harper & Row, 1986), *When Society Becomes an Addict* (Harper
& Row, 1987) and *The Addictive Organization*, co-authored with Diane Fassell
(Harper and Row, 1988).

that people in our society are addicted to, so she analyzed much of what is going on in the United States today in terms of its being an addictive society.

Schaef is describing in her books a victimization of the oppressors, slavery of the masters, the powerlessness of the powerful. The overwhelming majority of men in our society are addicted to ways of thinking, feeling and acting that systematically entrap them without their realizing it, in much the same way that alcohol, nicotine or other drug addictions subtly but securely ensnare their victims. They believe they are the lords of the social reality that they define, but actually they are imprisoned in it. The four walls of their prison cell are what Schaef calls four myths—overarching beliefs that define the mental world that most men live in.

The first myth is that *the white male system is the only thing that exists*. Men who are caught up in this system know no other way of looking at reality. They are addicted to a one-dimensional view of the world, and this defines reality for them. There is no other game in town but the game of power, status and wealth. It is the game that is played in the boardrooms of corporate America, on the stock and commodity exchanges, on the playing fields of professional sports, in local and national governments, in the ranks of factory and office workers and in the neighborhoods of suburbia. The list could be endlessly expanded because the myth embraces, in one way or another, everything in our lives. It is the way we all live. To one extent or another, we are all addicted to this system and to the reality it defines for us.

The second myth is that *the white male system is*

innately superior. Other people may have other ways of thinking, feeling and behaving, but they are out of touch with reality. Their attitudes and actions are at best quaint and amusing, and at worst wrong and threatening. From this position of superiority, those in the system can stand in judgment of those outside it. Women can be labeled as weak, blacks as incompetent, Chicanos as lazy, Russians as untrustworthy, the poor as unproductive, the uneducated as ignorant, the unborn as disposable. The list is as long as the list of white male prejudices. For the system defines what is right and good and true.

The third myth is that *the white male system knows and understands everything.* There is nothing that falls outside its purview or, if it does, it is unimportant. The system and those who dominate the system understand what is best for everybody and what is best for the world. They know what God wants, and they understand how God wants people to live. They can, therefore, legislate economy, policy and even morality. The system and those who are addicted to it have no doubts about the way things are and the way things ought to be.

The fourth myth is the belief that *it is possible to be totally logical, rational and objective.* Everything that is worth knowing is objectifiable and quantifiable. It can be counted as part of the gross national product, it can be measured and weighed in the balance of political power, it can be observed and analyzed by some science or another or it can be legislated or covered under some law or other. If there is something that cannot be known through the technology of the system, it is irrelevant and it can be disregarded. Feelings, values, hopes, ideals, rights and other intangibles only count when they can be quantified and measured.

Although the first three myths reveal how partial and incomplete the white male system really is, the fourth myth shows why it is so addictive. Like the alcoholic who engages in what Alcoholics Anonymous calls "stinkin' thinkin'," people caught up in this system engage in very limited thinking and perceiving. Their addiction to the system blinds them to anything and everything that falls outside the system. What they see and feel is only what feeds their addiction or what threatens it. To themselves they seem logical, even when they are being incoherent. To themselves they seem reasonable, even when they are being irrational. To themselves they seem moral, even when they are doing things that are destroying themselves and others.

Anne Wilson Schaef further suggests that these four myths are capped by yet another myth which they all support, much as the four walls of a cell support the ceiling that encapsulates the prisoner within it. Like the ceiling, no one pays much attention to it, but it is there. It is the belief that *it is possible for one to be God*. Most white males would, of course, deny that this is a part of their belief system, but that is because they do not look up to see what their beliefs ultimately lead to. If God is the one superior being who exists, who defines reality and who knows everything, then by creating and maintaining the addictive system white males are wittingly or unwittingly playing God.

I caught a glimpse of this when Bob Woodward wrote a book in which he questioned former CIA

Director William Casey's integrity to some extent.[5]

What is truly blasphemous is the replacement of God with the white male system, and the way that the system arrogates the attributes of God to itself. Call it patriotism, call it national self-interest, call it company loyalty or call it faithfulness to the Catholic Church, the demand for unquestioning allegiance and blind obedience is the same demand that a drug makes on an addict.

If people are to develop any deep spirituality today, and especially if men are to develop spiritually, they need to be liberated from self-serving worldviews. Mythologies usually represented this as the necessary killing of the dragon. Jesus calls it "blindness," and culpable blindness at that:

> Some of the Pharisees who were with him
> heard this and said to him, "Surely we are not
> also blind, are we?" Jesus said to them: "If you
> were blind, you would have no sin; but now
> you are saying, 'We see,' so your sin remains."
> (John 9:40-41)

---

[5]Woodward, Robert. *Veil: The Secret Wars of the CIA 1981-1987*. New York, N.Y.: Simon and Schuster, 1987. In an interview Casey's widow called Woodward's accusations blasphemous. If we can assume that Mrs. Casey, being an Irish Catholic, knows the correct meaning of blasphemy, then she would know that blasphemy can be committed only against God. Yet unconsciously she equated her husband with God.

4

The Two Journeys

Since we are beginning the journey of spiritual development without an inner map to guide us, we need to stop for a moment and see where we are, that is, where we are as products of our culture and as the sort of man that our society pictures as the typical male. Below is a possible map of the two journeys that many men are on today. You might study the pattern first before I further describe it in this chapter.

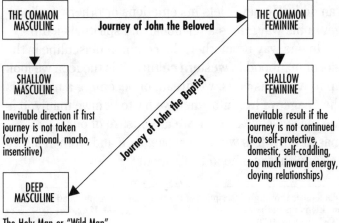

Let us call our starting off place, then, the common masculine. It is masculinity as it is commonly conceived, imagined and pictured in our society. It is the masculinity projected by John Wayne, James Bond and Rambo. It is the masculinity of the self-made man, the business tycoon, the entrepreneur. In politics it is the power broker and the decision-maker. In military dress it is the commander, the top soldier, the fighter. The cowboy and the sheriff, the cop and the detective, the explorer and the buccaneer—these figures and others of fiction and fact typify the common masculine.

The common masculine is all male, clear and through. There is nothing effeminate about him. He is a man's man. Other men respect him for his toughness, his prowess, his success. Women may adore him, fear him or want him, but they can never have him. He is the one who has them—his girlfriend, his wife, his mistress. He is his own man, and no one else's. He is independent and self-assured, intelligent and knowledgeable, resourceful and capable. If something needs doing, he can do it. He never lets his emotions or others' feelings get in his way. He is a relational and spiritual victim.

In one way or another, the common masculine is the idol of manhood in western culture. It is the icon we look up to when, as boys, we dream of becoming a man. It is the image we live into when we try to behave manly. It is the mask we wear when we are unsure of our masculinity. It is what everyone, men and women alike, assume that manhood is all about.[6]

---

[6]For a more thorough description of the common masculine, read the section on "Elements of the Male Role" in James A. Doyle, *The Masculine Experience* (W.C. Brown, 1983).

Yet if we are to develop spiritually, we must begin to move from this place to somewhere else. The common masculine is only the start of the spiritual journey.

♦ ♦ ♦

The first leg of that journey is a movement into the feminine. Although it was undoubtedly a factor in Jesus' own development as a man, we know very little about Jesus' life before his public ministry, so let us choose a different New Testament image for it. We shall name it the journey of John the Beloved, after the title that the writer of John's Gospel apparently gives himself, "the one whom Jesus loved" (John 13:23a).

At the Last Supper, this is the disciple who sat closest to Jesus and who, according to John's own account, rested his head on the breast of Jesus. Most men today would consider that socially unacceptable, and for most of us who are men it would be emotionally impossible. We just couldn't do it because it would look too effeminate or even homosexual. Yet this man was apparently quite comfortable in receiving affection and expressing emotion with others and even with another man. For this reason we might consider John the Beloved as the patron saint of the first journey in a man's spiritual development.

For most of us, the spiritual journey into the feminine begins through our relationships with women. As we learn how to relate to the women in our life—our mothers and grandmothers, our sisters and other female relatives, our girlfriends and eventually our wives—we discover that they inhabit a different space, as it were, than the common masculine. For want of a better name, let us call it the common feminine.

In terms of cultural stereotypes, the common feminine is just the opposite of what we described as the common masculine. Negatively, it is the femininity of the damsel in distress, the woman who needs to be rescued, guarded and protected by the male. Commonly in literature and in the media, she is the girlfriend, the wife, the mother of the hero, but she is never the hero. She is never the initiator, the doer, the decider; she is always the onlooker, the receiver of the male's attention and the beneficiary of his gifts. In fairy tales hers is the femininity of Cinderella, Snow White and Sleeping Beauty.

Even in the fairy tales, however, we also see a positive side to the common feminine. She is loving and caring, patient and industrious, graceful and charming. Even though she must wait for her virtue to be rewarded, she does everything she can to be worthy of the prince's attention. In the American stereotype she is the perfect hostess, the perfect wife, the perfect mother. She is attractive and imaginative, considerate and cooperative, supportive and helpful, gentle and nurturing. She is what girls have been traditionally taught to be and what boys have been told to expect in a woman.

As boys, we discover that the feminine reality is not our own, yet there is something fascinating and attractive about it. The feminine is something that we desire but, because we regard ourselves as purely male, we see the feminine as entirely outside us. Yet to attain the feminine, we must somehow enter into the world of the feminine and learn to speak its language. We must learn to be vulnerable and sensitive, we must watch our language and our manners, we must master the dance of courtship in order to obtain the object of our desire.

In this respect modern society has opened possibilities for the journey into the feminine which were not available in ancient and medieval times. When marriages were totally arranged (usually by the fathers of the bride and groom-to-be), boys did not have to learn the gentle arts of courtship. It was possible for men to postpone indefinitely the discovery of the feminine as anything that they could or should develop in themselves. Little did men realize that when they wrested the right to choose their own bride, they also gave women the right to be more selective about their own marriage partner. Slowly but surely, women are changing the cultural stereotype of the perfect husband.

Since the 1960's, other changes in our culture have also been making it both desirable and necessary for men to develop their feminine side. Besides the sexual revolution which has encouraged men and women to acknowledge one another as equals, the entrance of women into higher education and business in greater numbers has forced men to take womanhood more seriously. For the first time in history, men in great numbers have begun to question the validity and purpose of war and to break away from unquestioning patriotism. The social sciences of psychology and sociology have begun to understand the benefits of wholistic personal development and integrated life-styles. Literature, the arts and the media have begun to present images of the masculine that are not stereotypically male but more balanced by the female. It has become increasingly acceptable for men to develop the traditionally feminine strengths of listening and understanding, caring and nurturing. Alan Alda, Patrick Swayze and the Yuppie gentleman have replaced John Wayne.

I myself saw this happening firsthand during my thirteen years as pastor of the New Jerusalem community in Cincinnati. The community began in the early 1970's out of high school retreats for boys, but very quickly it began to include girls and married couples and older people as well. The majority, though, were young men and women, and quite naturally as one might expect, many of them fell in love with each other, got married and started raising families. By the mid-1980's most of these couples were raising their children, and one-half of the total community of four hundred were children and adolescents.

If you listen to the first tapes I made in the community,[7] you can hear me insisting again and again on the importance of conversion and surrender to God. In terms of masculinity and femininity I was talking about conversion from male attitudes of autonomy and control to more feminine attitudes of relationship and trust. At that time I saw the whole Christian journey in those terms because, quite frankly, that's where I was as a young priest in my own spiritual development, and that's certainly the direction in which the boys I was working with needed to grow. I was not yet aware that

---

[7]Many of these were published by St. Anthony Messenger Press, and *The Great Themes of Scripture* talks have also appeared in book form, available from the same publisher.

the girls might have needed to hear something very different, and that a woman's conversion might have to first take a turn toward the masculine, but that's what I was preaching and that's what the young men in the community were hearing.

As a group, then, the community moved in the direction of more feminine attitudes and living styles. We were all into listening and acceptance and affirmation and dialogue both at the community level and in families. The young men discovered a whole new world opening up for them, a world of receptivity and trust, revealing boundless possibilities for relating and parenting. They became very loving and nurturing fathers, quite different from many of the fathers they had grown up with.

At first we were all delighted with this, and the risks that the young men had taken in developing their feminine side seemed confirmed by their home life and legitimated by the community's experience of relative harmony. We did not suffer the kinds of rivalries and divisions that we heard other charismatic communities were going through. But gradually we began to hear about all sorts of problems arising in the homes as the children grew older. Slowly it dawned on us that part of the problem was that the children were being raised by two mothers, so to speak. The children had no experience of a strong masculine presence in the home.

Now, it's one thing for a man to get into his feminine side, but it's quite another to stay there—which is apparently what many of the young men in New Jerusalem were doing. No one could blame them, of course, because no one had ever told them that at some point their spiritual journey had to take a different turn.

We had all assumed, myself included, that spiritual development went more or less in a single direction. The reality of our own experience, though, was bringing us face-to-face with the shortsightedness of that view.

If a man succeeds in getting in touch with his femininity but then just stays in that space, his working self-image becomes something very close to what we have called the common feminine. It has, hopefully, all of the positive qualities of that paradigm, which is what we were promoting in the community, but invariably it brings with it many of the negative traits as well. Thus, we found ourselves with many young fathers who were woefully lacking in many of the paradigmatically masculine qualities of focus, determination, self-confidence and inner authority. Even into their late twenties, some of them were still looking outside themselves for direction, affirmation and even rescuing.

The cultural stereotype of the man who gets locked into the feminine side of his humanity is the wimp, the softie, the effeminate male. Let us name that the shallow feminine. It has no depth to it and no strength to it, especially when the negative aspects of the feminine override the positive aspects. By the late 1970's, we had many "good" but soft males in our society. They were likable, but to put it bluntly, they were not going to inspire or challenge anybody.

At a certain point in our community's spiritual pilgrimage, therefore, many of us began to become aware of some second step that needed to be taken by many of the young men, but we were still not sure what it should look like. Quite unexpectedly, the answer came to us from a feminist.

One day, Pat Brockman, the Ursuline sister who has been in the community since its inception, came into my office and showed me a book she had been reading by Betty Friedan titled *The Second Stage*.[8] Friedan's thesis was that up until then the women's movement had gone only halfway: It had freed women from male domination and it had allowed them to move into the masculine, but too often the result was that women who had so taken on the male stereotype were just as bad as the men they hated. What she was describing was the complete opposite of what had been happening to the men in New Jerusalem, but it was exactly parallel to it! Friedan was calling upon feminists to press further in their development as women in order to reach a deeper and more wholistic dimension of womanhood. Suddenly, it became clear to both Pat and me that the second stage needed by many of the men in our community was not more of the feminine but a turn to the masculine at a deeper level.

♦   ♦   ♦

Looking for a biblical image of this second journey, the journey into the deep masculine as we came to call it, I eventually decided to name it the journey of John the Baptist. In the Gospels this John is pictured as the complete opposite of John the Beloved. He is a wild man who lives alone on the edge of the desert, wearing coarse clothing and eating crude food. He knows all about people's sinfulness, so those who are willing to face it in themselves he calls to conversion, and those who are

---

[8]Friedan, Betty. *The Second Stage*. New York, N.Y.: Summit Books, 1982.

unwilling to face their own sinfulness he calls hypocrites and liars—whitewashed stinking tombs— and a pack of snakes. John doesn't mince words. He's not out to be a nice guy.

In order to maintain his integrity and forthrightness the Baptist deliberately leads a marginalized existence. He lives on the fringe of society, from where he can honestly tell it like it is. He doesn't wear what nice men are supposed to wear, so all he has is simple clothing made of camel's hair and leather. I don't suppose he took his suit to the dry cleaners, either. For food he lives on insects and wild honey. It's what the people in the desert, the ones who have been excluded from the mainstream of society, have to eat. To me, John the Baptist represents the wild side of God.

Christians forget that God in the Old Testament comes off much wilder than he does in the New Testament. Right at the beginning of the Bible in the Book of Genesis, he looks down from heaven and doesn't like the way people are living, so he decides to flood them out and start over again. That's wild! A little while later he picks out a guy named Abraham and tells him to pack up his stuff and head out for some place across the desert that he's never seen before. He tells Abraham and his wife, who are both about a hundred years old, that they're going to have a baby—and they do! But then he blows Abraham's mind by ordering him to sacrifice his only son, and this after telling him he will be the father of a great nation! This is an utterly free God trying to create spiritually free people.

We have so tamed the Scriptures that we don't see the wildness of God even when it's staring us in the face.

God goes around appearing to people in flaming bushes, in columns of smoke and fire, in clouds of thunder and lightning on mountain tops. The pharaoh of Egypt finds out the hard way how wild God is when he thinks his imperial building projects are more important than people's freedom. The Israelites, later on, think they've got it made because they're God's chosen people, but God smashes their own petty kingdom for not living up to what he chose them for. God is not a "company man" and does not appear to be calling for company or tribal values. Yahweh is the God of "all the peoples" and forms his own "rainbow coalition."

The prophets, too, were a wild bunch. They had to be because they were the spokesmen of a wild God, a God who didn't care much about temples and offerings but who cared a lot about the way people were treated. Read your Bible, it's all there. We tend to think the prophets were fortune-tellers predicting the Christian future, but they were much more, naming the ever-present illusions. They were non-clergy with a radical message from a dangerous God and for their efforts all they got was turned off, persecuted and killed (see Matthew 23:29-36). Down to the last of the prophets, John the Baptist, domesticated religion is always threatened by people of universal integrity.

So John, the archetypal wild man, is the perfect patron saint for the second leg of the journey, the journey toward the deep masculine. It's a hard journey to hear about, and an even harder one to make.

This spiritual journey into the deep masculine is difficult to hear about because it is all too easy to misunderstand what is said about it. So much of what the

Baptist represents can be mistaken for the independent tough guy, the crude macho hero, which is in reality the shallow (negative) masculine. If you haven't at least begun the first journey, you'll have no idea at all what the second journey is really about, and you will tend to hear it as a confirmation of the common masculine. If the journey of John the Beloved can be characterized as a movement into and integration of the feminine, the journey of John the Baptist has to be thought of as a movement from the feminine back into the masculine, and a new reintegration of the two.

The whole journey, the full development of the male spirit, has to walk in the steps of both Johns, not just of one of them. The basic reason why the journey of the second John is hard to make is because if you stick your neck out your head may wind up on somebody else's platter, which, of course, is what happened to the Baptist. It is a risky journey, just as much as the inner movement into the feminine is, but it is a journey back out into the external world—into the world of risk, uncertainty and almost certain failure. No wonder many prefer to remain safely in the world of ideas and opinions.

In my own personal experience and in the experience of many of the men I've worked with, there seems to be a natural time sequence for making the two journeys. During the first twenty years or so of our life we spend most of our energy just appropriating the common masculine. During our teenage years especially, we struggle so hard to become what we think it means to be a man, whereas in reality we're only just constructing the base camp from which our spiritual trek can begin. We don't see that at the time, of course.

If we are unlucky—and most of the men in our society fall into this misfortune—we think we've arrived, and we spend the rest of our life in the shallow masculine. But if somehow we encounter the feminine— in a woman, in the poor, in religion, or wherever—and we realize we need to grow in that direction, we spend the next twenty years or so courting the eternal feminine, trying to please women and searching for our own inner souls.

Around age forty or forty-five, men hit a mid-life crisis which is sometimes called the male menopause. For those of us who have been stuck in the shallow masculine up till then, we seem to get hit with a blow to our masculine ego which Jung and other psychologists say is the feminine in us making a last-ditch effort to break into our consciousness, lest we move into the last half of our life only half developed psychically. For those of us who have made it into our feminine side, however, the jolt hits what we thought was our well-integrated psyche. Instead of being bothered by our unconscious feminine potential, we find ourselves being disturbed by our unrealized masculine potential.

I do not want to convey the impression, however, that everything happens in neat twenty-year cycles. This is just a schematic way of looking at typical male spiritual development, which seems to have some validity for a good number of men. In real life there is no such thing as an average spiritual journey; each man's is unique.

The other impression I do not want to convey is that the first journey has to be fully completed before the second journey is begun. Talking about spiritual development as a journey is a simple image for a highly complex developmental task. We never get it all together, not even the first part of it. Becoming psychically whole through the integration of the feminine is a lifelong task in itself. It is never fully completed, and we are always discovering aspects of the shallow masculine in ourselves which need to be confronted, converted and complemented by the feminine in ourselves. To put off moving in the direction of John the Baptist because we are still moving in the direction of John the Beloved means nothing less than getting stuck in the shallow (negative) feminine.

If there is a real pitfall in the road to masculine spirituality today, this is where it lies. So much is being written about allowing and encouraging men to develop their feminine side that it is very easy to mistake the first leg of the journey for the whole odyssey. Part of the difficulty, of course, is that in our western culture and even in our religious tradition we have few guides to lead us deeply into the masculine and almost no mentors who have been there and come back to guide us. We are longing for mentors on the male journey.

Interestingly enough, our word "mentor" comes from Greek mythology. Mentor was the wise and trusted counselor of Odysseus. When Odysseus went on his long journey, he put Mentor in charge of his son Telemachus as his teacher and the guardian of his soul. It seems that one's father is seldom the initiator of the son. It is always another special man who must guide the boy into manhood. (Perhaps much of our problem today is not just that we have so few "godfathers," but that we expect from our biological fathers far too much!)

A final fascinating twist is that some saw Mentor as a disguise for Athena, the feminine goddess of wisdom and war. In other words, the only trustworthy guide for Telemachus is a man with the spirit of a woman, who is herself both warrior and wisdom. The ancients understood that to be a man, the boy must both break with the feminine and yet be led back into it. We see Jesus doing the same when he leaves his mother to sit among the doctors in the temple, listening to them and asking them questions (see Luke 2:46). When questioned by Mary, he does not hesitate to say that he must be about the affairs of his Father (see Luke 2:49). Yet he returned to his mother's house and only eighteen years later feels ready to speak publicly of God. The ancients and the Scriptures were far more aware than we of stages, timing and necessary journeys.

In men's work we speak of the uninitiated man as the *puer* (the Latin word for boy or child). If we have many *puers* today, it is not only because we have little knowledge of the rather universal initiation rites for young men but also because we have so few mentors and guides on those journeys. Who will go first?

Mere bosses, coaches and teachers tell a young man how to get out of his problems. A true mentor guides him *into* them and *through* them. Trust the two Johns to do the same.

5

Men's Liberation

"There are two ways of being a prophet. One
is to tell the enslaved that they can be free. It
is the difficult path of Moses. The second is to
tell those who think they are free that they are
in fact enslaved. This is the even more difficult
path of Jesus."

—Richard Rohr

My very first assignment as a deacon was with the
Acoma Indian tribe in New Mexico. Before I drove to
visit them, the other Franciscans tried to prepare me for
a culture shock by telling me how different these people
are. They said that the Acoma are a matriarchal society
in which the women are the real leaders of the tribe. It is
the women who are strong, who make the decisions and
who tell the men what to do. If I wanted to work with
these people, I was advised, I would have to learn to
work with the women.

Thus forewarned, I spent my initial time at the
reservation just observing and listening, trying to learn
the social patterns that prevailed among the Acoma.

After a few weeks, however, it dawned on me that there wasn't much difference between these people and the folks back home. The only thing that was different was that the Acoma were honest about the way their society works. The women have power and everyone admits it, whereas in white society everyone pretends that men are in charge. We men think we call the shots, but many of the day-to-day decisions that control our lives are made by women.

An anecdote I read somewhere conveys this idea humorously but pointedly. When asked who makes the decisions in his family, a man replied that his wife makes all the little decisions and she lets him make all the big decisions. Pressed to clarify what he meant by that, he explained, "My wife decides what neighborhood we should live in, what schools are best for the children, how to budget our money, where we should go on vacation and things like that. But I decide the big issues, like whether we should trust the Russians, whether the government is doing a good job and what we should do about the economy." The story is both funny and sad because the man has obviously been hoodwinked into believing that he has any real decisionmaking power.

Even on the job, most men do not have much power. If they are blue-collar workers, they do what they are told to do, which is usually the same thing over and over again every day. If they are supervisors or managers, there is always some boss higher up telling them what to do and what not to do. If they are salespeople, they are always trying to please their customers. Even if they are executives, most of their so-called decisions are determined by still higher executives, by boards of directors and by market forces beyond their control. Most men are paid for doing what someone else wants done. They do not really control their own lives. No wonder so many men have become passive.

This lack of control is why entertainment and vacation are so important in our culture. The stresses of always meeting someone else's deadlines, of living up to someone else's expectations and of knowing that another man is ready to step into his job if he performs poorly make it necessary to periodically get out of the rat race and forget how tense he is. So he can't really decide not to watch television or not to go out on the weekend or not to take a vacation because he needs those escapes from his daily grind. Our culture presents men with the illusion of making decisions, but it effectively castrates them from charting actual new directions beyond and outside of the rat race. Men hardly ever have a chance to make decisions that make a real difference in their own lives or in the world around them. They have to play the game or they won't be rewarded.

Another indication of this is how few people in America bother to vote. On the surface, we pride ourselves on our democracy, but less than half the eligible voters turn out for national elections and even fewer than that bother to vote in local elections. The president of the United States, for instance, is regularly elected by only about a quarter of the adults in our country. When questioned by pollsters, many Americans say they do not vote because they feel powerless to change the system or because they see no real difference between the candidates. No matter who wins, they say, the real decisions in the government will be controlled by powerful lobbies and business interests. They do not bother to write Congress or to join citizens' action groups for essentially the same reasons.

The white male system, therefore, offers the illusion of power while holding back any real decisionmaking power. This is also why it must offer illusions of success—promotions, paychecks and other symbols of prestige—to men who subconsciously know that moving to another niche in the maze is no escape from the totally controlling game they are forced to play. A larger desk, a private office, a bigger house, a newer car, a more expensive vacation—such are the essentially empty rewards men receive for surrendering their freedom and draining their masculine energy in the service of the system.

Men are taught the rules of the system quite early in their lives. When I was teaching in Roger Bacon High School in Cincinnati, most of the boys were what you would call normal. They were smart but not brilliant, they were average looking but not terrifically handsome, and they were healthy but not the best athletes. And yet the overwhelming majority of them felt bad about themselves. If they couldn't be elected to the student senate, if they didn't look like movie stars, if they couldn't make the football team, they felt like they were nothing. You'd hope that a Franciscan boys' school would offer them a more Christian outlook on life, but it operated on the same set of values that the world works on. Catholic education, like all education in our culture, teaches the motivations and rewards of the white male system in which the individual is always blamed for failure, never the system itself.

Part of our oppression as men, of course, is that we are taught to oppress others who have less status than we do. We especially oppress racial minorities, homosexuals, the poor and women. Psychologically (in the slave psychology of the white male system) we have to do this in order to have some feeling of superiority in the absence of any real accomplishments. When we are prevented from making any actual difference in the world, we create illusions of difference in order to have any self-esteem at all.

Men's liberation is, therefore, even more difficult than women's liberation. Women know that they are oppressed, and that in itself is the beginning of liberation. Women know the games men play, whereas we men do not even recognize the system as a set of games. Even when we do recognize it, we believe that that's simply the way the world is, the way life has to be, because the white male system has defined reality for us. But it is not the way life has to be. There *is* a way out of the system—a way, as Jesus puts it, that is not of this world.

In biblical language the way is called salvation: being saved from the world and its false promises. In the mythic language of the folktale the way is pictured as freeing the wild man. In the language of psychology the way is to release the creative energy of the deep masculine. In the language of spirituality the way is the twofold journey of John the Beloved and John the Baptist. In theological language the way is entering into the mystery of the Trinity, discovering that we are made in the image and likeness of God and participating in the work of redemption.[9]

Through the efforts of the women's liberation movement, many women are further along the road to salvation than men are. Women have recognized their oppression, they have named it, and they have begun a conscious journey into the masculine side of their androgynous selves. But even if they are not consciously part of the women's liberation movement, they are already drawing upon their masculine energy to organize the home, to keep the family moving, to get things done.

Ironically, women wield much of the power in our patriarchal society, at the day-to-day level where many real-life decisions are made. Some women do not recognize this, but most men do not even suspect it. Most men are so fascinated by what passes for masculinity in our culture that they have not even begun to move into their feminine side. Most men are so trapped in the games of the white male system that they do not even sense a need for liberation. Most men are not even angry that the institutions which manipulate their lives have psychologically castrated them and cut them off from their own deep masculinity.

Men's liberation is therefore more difficult and more necessary than women's liberation. It is more difficult because most of us do not know that we need to be liberated. And it is more necessary because our enslavement is keeping the whole system going. The lonely, unhealthy and addictive character of men's lives

---

[9]The concepts alluded to in this paragraph will be developed at greater length in subsequent sections. They are mentioned together here so that you can see that they are all interrelated.

is too high a price to pay to maintain this patriarchal culture.

I often feel, as Thomas Merton did, like a conductor on a train heading toward a certain cliff. You run up and down the aisles telling the people to get off before it is too late, and they only gawk in wonder at your obvious incoherence. You cannot liberate anybody until they are convinced they need liberation. In poorer cultures this is somewhat easy. Here, in our culture, we have just enough middle-class comfort to avoid the question for an awfully long time—sometimes forever.

6

Male Initiation

"The heroes of all time have gone before us;
the labyrinth is thoroughly known; we have
only to follow the thread of the hero path. And
where we had thought to find an abomination,
we shall find a god; where we had thought to
travel outward, we shall come to the center of
our own existence; and where we had thought
to be alone, we shall be with all the world."

—Joseph Campbell[10]

In almost all cultures men are not born—they are made.
Much more than for women, cultures have traditionally
demanded puberty and initiation rites for the boys. It is
almost as if the biological experiences of menstruation
and childbirth are enough wisdom for women, but
invariably men must be tried, limited, challenged,
punished, hazed, circumcised, isolated, starved, stripped
and goaded into maturity. The pattern is nearly
universal, and the only real exceptions are the recent

---

[10]As quoted by Leonard Biallas in *Myths, Gods, Heroes, and Saviours*. Mystic,
Conn.: Twenty-Third Publications, 1986, p. 166.

secular West. Boy Scouts, Confirmation classes, Lions and Elks clubs have tried to substitute, but with little spiritual effect.

Historically, the program was clear. The boy had to be separated from protective feminine energy, led into ritual space where newness and maleness could be experienced as holy; the boy had to be ritually wounded and tested, and experience bonding with other men and loyalty to tribal values. The pattern is so widely documented that one is amazed that we have let go of it so easily. The contemporary experience of gangs, gender identity confusion, romanticization of war, aimless violence and homophobia will all grow unchecked, I predict, until boys are again mentored and formally taught by wise elders. Historically, it was much of the meaning of the medicine man, the priest and the shaman. Now boys look to coaches, drill sergeants and fundamentalist preachers for what the Church no longer gives them. In fact, they even resent it from clergymen, probably because we too long gave them stones instead of bread, moral minimals instead of courageous journeys, holy days of obligation instead of risky vision quests.

Male initiation always has to do with hardness, difficulty, struggle and usually a respectful confrontation with the non-rational, the unconscious or, if you will, the wild. It prepares the young man to deal with life in other ways than logic, managing and problem solving. Frankly, it prepares him for the confrontation with Spirit.

Because we have no such training today, the modern male is not only trapped inside his comfort zone, but he is also trapped inside of his psyche and what he thinks is reason. This is the myth of modernism, which has surrounded the last hundreds of years in the West. It is a myth just as surely as was the myth of Zeus or the myth of Quetzalcoatl or the myth of Adam and Eve. Because our men have not been initiated into the sacred, they think their myth is actually objective truth and universal order. They are so trapped inside of the myth of modernism (philosophy of progress + left-brain reason as truth + autonomy and development of the individual) that we are less and less capable of encountering Transcendent Reality. Secularism, in this sense, is at the bottom of most contemporary disbelief. Atheism and agnosticism were unthinkable until the modern period. They are still unthinkable for wisely initiated men.

In classic "salvation stories" and mythic journeys men typically move through several levels of consciousness: from simple to complex to enlightened. There are much finer distinctions within these, but for our purposes here, these three will suffice. It matches the advice of the Zen master who says to start with the common sense answer, then think, study, wait, struggle and search as if it all depended on you, and it will lead you back to the common sense answer, but in a whole new way that is not common sense at all.

The *puer*, or uninitiated male, starts in simple consciousness. Everything is wondrous and true, black and white, filled with mystery and meaning right beneath the surface. We are true believers until about age seven or eight, although many folks are able to retain simple consciousness much longer. It is an innocence ("un-woundedness") that many people in protected families and uncomplicated societies enjoy for much of their lives. It is naive, and often dangerous, but is characterized by a rich inner life of stories, meanings and clear reference points that allow people to walk through great difficulty unscathed. They just go inside and find their transcendent purpose, and all injustices, contradictions and sufferings can be dealt with. It is the divine therapy that has carried most people through life since the beginning of time. It is quite simply called belief or faith. It works like nothing else. It is Adam and Eve in the garden, at one with themselves, the animals, creation and God.

But we have to leave the garden to write the rest of the Bible. We invariably eat of the tree of the knowledge of good and evil and move into complex consciousness. We get educated, start thinking, managing and trying to control the data. We become a mass of contradictions and opinions, and helpful denials. We know the answer is out there somewhere, and we keep listening for answers, reading books and hunkering down with pro tem certitudes until the next anxiety attack.

This is most of the journey, amidst Scylla and Charybdis, the Minotaur and the Sirens. It is the Israelites wandering in circles for forty days in the desert. It is the modern, educated liberal thinker looking for final truth in feelings, explanations and political correctness. In complex consciousness we know too much to go back to the garden, symbolized by the cherubs with flaming swords that guard the return to the tree of life (see Genesis 3:24).

But we do not know enough to be enlightened. It is the angst and the burden of modern men. They are trapped in complex consciousness and keep returning to the same wells for water: the wells of reason, order, control and power. It is good, necessary and predictable. Without the second stage there is no desire, no spaciousness, no real understanding of the gift. Normally the hero never passes through to enlightenment until he has sustained a number of wounds, disappointments and paradoxes. It is the struggle with darkness and grief that educates the male soul. Physically that darkness is experienced as pain and handicap, like the wounded hip of Jacob (Genesis 32:26). Intellectually the darkness and absurdity of things is faced by riddles and koans,[11] like the question of the Sphinx or the non-answers of the Zen master. I am convinced that much of Jesus' Sermon on the Mount is the same, but the western Church had no patience to deal with his wisdom, which is from the enlightened third stage.

If we are willing to be led, we are led toward enlightenment. The hero cannot really intend, choose or even fully decide for enlightenment. He does not know what it is yet! All he can do is be *ready* for it! All of life is readying, attuning, awakening. Note how many of Jesus' parables and teachings are about being ready and awake. The easiest substitute, of course, is religion. It substitutes answers and too easy certitude about past and future for *simple present awareness*. Strange as it seems, religion commonly avoids true enlightenment. It shows itself in tribal, narrow thinking, more based in fear and control than the daring search for God.

---

[11]A paradox to be meditated upon that is used to train Zen Buddhist monks to abandon ultimate dependence on reason and to force them into gaining sudden intuitive enlightenment (*Webster's Ninth New Collegiate Dictionary*, 1985).

Enlightenment is not so much knowing as unknowing; it is not so much learning as unlearning. It is a second and chosen naiveté, without fully forgetting all the contradictions and complexity in between. It is more surrendering than concluding, more trusting than fixing and more gratuitous grace than anything. You cannot get yourself enlightened by any known program, ritual or moral practice. This drives the religionists crazy, but as Jesus said, the Spirit blows wherever it pleases (see John 3:8). All you can do is stay on the journey, listen to its lessons, both agony and ecstasy, and ask for that most rare and crucial of gifts: openness. All we can really do is to keep ourselves out of the way (usually symbolized by the killing of the dragon in mythology) and ask that we will recognize the secret doorway out of complexity. When we stop knocking at that door, it will be because we realize we have been knocking from the inside.

It is the lost task of spirituality to keep us on this journey to tell men in particular that there even is such a journey.

➤➤➤ **7** ◄◄◄

Separation—Encounter—Return

"Whom does the Grail serve?"
—Parsifal's crucial question
after completing the quest

The journey toward the wild man or wise man finds amazingly uniform patterns in the heroes' actions of universal mythologies. The hero might have a thousand paths to walk, but there seem to be classic and constant patterns beneath his meanderings. Barry Lopez mirrors my own belief when he says that the truth can be found by looking for a discernible pattern.[12] It is *no* surprise that *the* essential mystery of faith for Catholic Christians is not a credal statement as much as a Christ-revealed *pattern*: Christ has died, Christ is risen and Christ will come again. Life will be death, failure and absurdity; life will be renewal, joy and beauty; and this pattern is inevitable, universal and salvific. Jesus for us is the ultimate mythmaker who reveals the way things work, and thereby tells us we can trust and expect this same

---

[12]Barry Lopez. *Crossing Open Ground.* New York, N.Y.: Charles Scribner's Sons, 1988, p. 69.

path. Before Jesus' ultimate life statement, culture after culture was being taught by the same Spirit and about the same pattern.

First of all, it is rather common to speak of two births that are necessary to come to enlightenment. The first is natural and biological; the second we must be initiated into. It is not certain that it will happen. Thus the great religious leaders speak urgently of the necessity of conversion, choice, search and surrender. Before we are "born again" we basically do not understand. We are either innocent, cynical or trapped in passing images. The East calls it blindness, illusion or aimless desire; the Christian West tends to call this once-born state sin. This is quite clear, for example, in the writings of St. Paul. Sin is much more a state of consciousness (or unconsciousness!) than it is individual immoral actions. Without the spiritual journey, we have the backwards phenomenon of people who supposedly avoid sins but are still in the state of sin! They don't cuss, drink or run around, but do so from a totally unenlightened consciousness that is usually based on fear or social convention. My point is: the journey, the path, the pattern are essential. What happens on that path is in some ways arbitrary and yet providential. It's all what we do with it.

Out of a formless, uninitiated life there comes *a call*. The hero is somehow directed beyond the private self on a search, an adventure, toward some transcendent goal. This call can come from within or by the example and circumstances of without, but the would-be hero is enticed by Otherness, by Mystery, by the Holy. This is the first stage of re-birth. It is the threshold experience and at this point our yes takes many forms, but there must be a clear recognition and a clear yes. Many are unfortunately hesitant at this stage. There is no one to tell them what this longing means, where it comes from and where it is leading. How much we are missing because there are so few spiritual directors and guides today!

Thus we usually find that the journey continues when there is a *protective figure* encountered, who aids, encourages and gives strength and direction to the would-be hero. The journey never happens alone. There is always a wise elder, a guardian angel, a patron saint, a father figure who both teaches the direction of the journey and warns of the dangers and obstacles that will be encountered along the way. Usually there are many demons and dragons to be faced, but only one clear guiding figure. The negative has many faces, the positive is usually presented as clear, simple and beautiful— although still mysterious. The common pattern today is to eclectically choose from many traditions and teachers before one has been followed decisively. It usually goes nowhere because the keeper of the gate is the protective ego, who decides when and if he is going to surrender.

So the *threshold experience* normally happens when one's own system of logic, meaning and truth break down. As Carl Jung said, a true encounter with the Numinous is *always* an annihilation for the ego! It's when Perseus confronts the serpented head of Medusa; it's when Jesus feels betrayed by Peter, Judas, the crowds and finally his own Father; it's when the modern man faces his shadow head-on by failure, imprisonment or accusation. For the man to be born, the boy must die.

The difficulty with an affluent culture like our own is that "infantile grandiosity" can be maintained well into late life by money, meddling or moving away. Quite simply, there is no room for God within us as long as we are filled with our false selves. As Jesus said, unless the grain of wheat dies, it remains just a grain of wheat (see John 12:24).

As the cocoon of the false self is let go, the true self stands revealed. The true self knows who it is, what it must do and, most excitingly, has the energy to do it—no matter what the price. This is *the task* itself, the sense of vocation, the sense of goal, purpose and challenge that guides every hero's life. Quite simply, a hero is one who gives his life to something bigger than himself. He goes for something and is not just along for the ride, but that something must be larger than his own life. We have grown very cynical about the possibility of true heroes. Feathering your own nest has become so acceptable that we largely substitute celebrities for heroes. Now you are a "hero" if you make a million dollars, and a fool if you give it away. To turn around the classic hero's journey in favor of self-interest puts us at odds with almost all known literature, legend and oral tradition. It certainly puts us at odds with Jesus, Buddha, Abraham and all the prophets. When a man cannot do greatness in some real sense, his life has no universal significance or transcendent meaning. He is disconnected with the "love that moves the sun and the other stars," as Dante said. In that sense, his life is a disaster, literally "disconnected from the stars."

If you read spiritual stories closely, you will see that there is always *a task within the task*, a struggle alongside the struggle. It is not enough to kill the dragon, save the maiden or even die on the cross. The real hero's task is to keep humor, to find soul, to maintain freedom, to discover joy, to expand vision in the process of killing dragons! There is no room for pettiness or petulance or self-pity, or one is not a hero. The sour saint is no saint at all. Our real demons are interior, quiet and disguised and often show themselves as the noonday devil—that pride, negativity or self-absorption that reveals itself in midlife and spoils the seeming good fruit of early accomplishments. Without spiritual disciplines and regular repentance, far too many of us win many battles but finally lose the war. How utterly sad it has been in my work to meet retired, bitter bishops, sad but "successful" priests and angry old widowers blaming the world for their loneliness. They had no Sancho Panza to accompany them, it seems, as they tilted at life's windmills.

The final stages of the monomyth are the issues of return. The hero typically receives some kind of *gift* or holy grail at the end of his quest. Don Quixote is forever searching for the "bread that is better than wheat." Prometheus receives fire, Solomon receives wisdom, Jason the golden fleece and Jesus hands over the Spirit. Often the hero receives the eternal feminine in the person of a fair maiden or queen or princess. The holy marriage is completed when they become one and live happily ever after. The kingdom is now healthy and fertile because the masculine and the feminine have become one new reality. But the important thing is that the gift is given over for others. The grail is not for power, prestige or private possession. It is always for the sake of the community, for the common good. I am afraid to wonder if we even understand this stage anymore. Far too often our concern seems to be IRAs, self-serving politics and playing golf in Florida. No civilization has ever survived unless the elders saw it their duty to pass on gifts of spirit to the young ones. Is it that we are selfish or is it that we ourselves have never found the gift? I suspect it is largely the latter.

There are no loners among the great heroes. There are no self-made men who clean up the town and ride off into the sunset. It is always obvious in the stories that many characters, advisors and circumstances have formed them by the end—usually in spite of themselves. What the pagan mythologies would have seen as fate or destiny, Christian stories would see as grace or Providence. But in either case the hero is formed and created by his times and his struggles and, most of all, by his enemies. He has never created himself. In the final paragraphs of the story, the hero invariably *returns home*, back to his community. He rejoins the folk with his tranforming gift. Odysseus must return to Ithaca, the saints must help us here on earth, Jesus says they will meet him not in imperial Jerusalem but on the humble roads of Galilee. Finally, the hero is a hero precisely because he knows how to re-integrate within the community.

Enlightened consciousness, looked at externally, looks amazingly like simple consciousness. Second naiveté can be confused with first by the uninitiated. The sayings of wise and wild men look harmless and irrelevant to those trapped in the complex middle. The end of a wisdom journey looks like the beginning:

> "And the end of all our exploring
> Will be to arrive where we started
> And know the place for the first time."[13]

---

[13]Eliot, T. S. "Little Gidding," *The Complete Poems and Plays, 1909-1950*. New York, N.Y.: Harcourt Brace Jovanovich, Inc., 1971, p. 145.

8

Man the Maker

Until the last century, men spent most of their time making and producing things. The majority of men were farmers, planting, cultivating and reaping the fruits of their labors in ways very tangible and down to earth. Many men were also craftsmen and builders. They made things that had form and meaning which made their world livable, which gave it beauty and which enriched the community in which they lived. Men worked with their hands and their heads and their hearts to produce the tangible goods of human culture, and they could see in the products of their work the good they were doing for themselves and others.

In our highly technological society, more and more men are no longer engaged in the traditionally masculine enterprise of making things. Instead, they are engaged in the business of making money. They move from one job to the next, even from one career to the next, all in the interest of making more money. They have little or no investment in the goods they are making or the services they are offering. Making money is not only the bottom line, it is the entire ledger.

This is a drastic shift in the orientation of men vis-à-vis the world they live in. A recent survey of boys in the eighth grade of grammar school revealed that ninety percent of them see their primary goal in life as "making lots of money." Not falling in love and raising a family, not inventing or discovering something new, not exploring the secrets of nature, not making the world a better place, but simply making money—and lots of it.

In magazines and newspapers I occasionally read stories about men who make thousands of dollars—even tens of thousands of dollars—just by making phone calls. They are playing the stock market or dealing in commodities futures or trading real estate, and in a matter of seconds they are able to make what every schoolboy wants to make: lots of money. On the one hand, that's very interesting because it reveals something about how the white male system works. But on the other hand, it's scary because it reveals even more about our cultural values.

It is especially frightening in the area of spirituality. In a very real sense the man who is engaged in making money is not making anything at all. Money is a fiction created to facilitate the exchange of goods and services. It is a something that is really nothing—literally, no thing. It is, from the perspective of spirituality, an illusion. Money is a game of numbers used to bolster a false self image and to perpetuate a false impression of power.

As we have already seen, masculine energy is naturally directed outward. For untold thousands of years that male energy has been directed outward to the world, toward making and producing things, toward creating and sustaining and improving life. In terms of sexuality it can be called phallic energy because one of the basic male drives is toward intercourse and the begetting of children. The great psychologist, Sigmund Freud, believed that civilization itself was the product of phallic energy that had been sublimated and directed toward things other than sex. Whether or not we agree with Freud, we can see that male sexual energy and male productive energy are both directed outward.

In today's western culture, however, men's energies are hardly directed toward the creation of life and the production of real things. Another famous psychologist (and pupil of Freud), Carl Jung, has suggested that the outer world is a blank screen onto which we project the inner life of the soul. If this is true, then today the soul of the western male is almost entirely projected onto a fiction—onto money, which is an empty symbol of prestige and power.

Money is an empty symbol precisely because it stands for anything and everything besides the paper or metal it is made of. Money has no inherent meaning, which is why it can take any projection that we want to put on it. Besides this, the paper and metal in themselves are practically worthless. This then is why directing one's life toward the making of money is so dangerous. It is a life commitment to making what is inherently meaningless and worthless, yet onto it we project all sorts of value and importance.

Up through the Middle Ages in Europe coins were never a common commodity, and most people simply exchanged goods and services. In the Renaissance, after the invention of printing, paper money made its first appearance. There is an interesting story of how when some friars proudly showed St. Francis of Assisi some money that had been donated to the order, he took it in his mouth, refused to touch it, walked out to the latrine and dropped it in. Francis saw that it was worthless, but more than that, he wanted to dispel the false impression that by collecting it the friars had done anything to be proud of. Even today, monks in Buddhist monasteries are forbidden to receive gifts of money in any form. They only accept contributions in the form of real things— food, cloth, pottery, wood and so on. Strange to say, but some Buddhists practice the spiritual lesson that Francis wanted to teach, and we Franciscans do not.

Please don't get me wrong. I am not advocating that all Franciscans, or all Christians for that matter, should immediately give away all their money and have nothing to do with it. I am simply pointing out that great spiritual masters of the past, including Jesus and Buddha and Francis, warned against the idolization of money. It is all too easy to fall in love with money, to be captivated by the pursuit of money and to project every manner of meaning and value onto money. If money is not explicitly placed under the reign of God, it will never be neutral for long. It will demand allegiance. Those who want to develop spiritually need to be very, very careful in the way they look at money and work with it. There is no reason to believe that the demon of money has been exorcized until it has been consciously named, rebuked and replaced by something better, I would hope something real.

9

Man the Aggressor

Men are often aggressive. They seem to have an inborn need to fight, to put themselves in conflict with the outer world in order to test themselves and to conquer it.

Is this need really inborn, or is it something that men learn? Does it come from their genes or from their environment? Psychologists today are still arguing on both sides of that issue. My point is, however, that it is an issue.[14]

Even studies of children seem to bear out this tendency. When given blocks of clay to play with, girls will more often make rounded, circling, enclosing, protecting, womb-like things, whereas boys will more often make straight, tall, intruding, projecting, phallus-like things. Who teaches them to do that?

Which of you, when you were a boy, did not kick a can down a sidewalk or boot a rock down a street? Which of you did not pick up a stone and heave it, either at some target or just to see how far you could throw it? Which of

---

[14]Richard's characterizations of men in contemporary America are corroborated in James A. Doyle, *The Male Experience* (W.C. Brown, 1983), chapters 7-11.

you never jumped in a puddle, just because it was there? Which of you never played with swords and guns made of sticks or manufactured? Which of you never climbed up into a tree, or explored a cave, to see how far you could go? We men are like that.

Some girls and women are like that, too. But we are talking here about the majority of *men*, and about the typical male, in trying to understand the male psyche and develop a masculine spirituality. That means we first of all have to understand our own nature, our basic orientation. We have to come to terms with where we are before we can think about we are going spiritually.

Why are we men like that? One commonly accepted theory in developmental psychology is that it comes from (or is reinforced by) the uniquely male task of separating ourselves from our mothers. Female infants do not have to face this task until much later in life, during their adolescence when they have to establish their own identity as a woman different from their mother. As boys, however, we have to face it fairly early in our development.

All infants begin their life in the maternal womb. Then, during the first few months and years of the infant's life, the mother's tenderness and caring become an extension of that womb-like, nurturing environment. Somewhere along the line, though, we begin to notice that we are not like mom. We have a penis, and she has breasts. We wear pants, and she wears skirts. She tells us that we are like daddy, that we will grow up to be like daddy. So at a very early age we begin to understand that we have to look outward, away from mommy, to become what we are supposed to be.

Too often, however, daddy is not around very much. Mommy is usually the one who is most often there when we need feeding, washing, clothing, comforting. Having been told that we are not like mommy, we slowly pull away from our initial closeness to her and seek closeness to someone else. But he is not there, not nearly enough. We are unable to develop the relationship patterns and skills that girls typically develop very early and retain throughout their life. We have to find someone or something else to project our developmental energies into. We project ourselves outward, into things.

For the rest of our life, we live with that early-acquired outward orientation. We move out from the womb, out from the home, into the world of television and comic books, playthings and playmates, games and sports, schools and clubs, business and politics, to make something of ourselves and find the meaning of our lives. Intimacy comes hard to us, and to some of us it hardly comes at all. It seems we are better at separation than at union. We make our way through life aggressively pushing at the world around us, stretching ourselves to the limit. But the limits, when we come against them, are almost invariably outside ourselves.

As men, then, we are not born or trained to discover and explore our inner world, the space of our psyche, our soul, our spirit. Again, of course, I am speaking in generalities, for there are certainly men who are naturally introvertive, contemplative, sensitive, creative and artistic. Most of us, though, come only slowly to the discovery of the spirit within us and to the realization that our spirit is in need of development.

The same can be said about relationships.

Relationships are spiritual realities, not objects in the world of things. Even though there is always someone out there to whom we are relating, discovering and developing a relationship that is more than a casual acquaintance or a working partnership is an inner spiritual task, not an outer accomplishment. It requires that we be in touch with our own feelings and that we be sensitive to the intangible feelings of the other person. It demands introspection, self-knowledge and self-reflection. It may even demand self-control, self-development and even change in our inner self—our thoughts, feelings and attitudes. Yet our life as boys does not well prepare us for those demands.

One of the first tasks of male spirituality, therefore, is to come to terms with what we are and to realize that what we have become ill equips us for what we have yet to become. For we have to learn to journey inward if we are ever to find ourselves and if we are ever to encounter God. We have to find our center.

In a sense we are a circumference people, with little access to the center of our own being. We live on the boundaries of our lives, confusing edges with essence, too quickly claiming the superficial as substance, believing that what we see at the edges is essential to our happiness.

It's not that what we find around us is bad. If the circumferences of our lives were evil, they would be easier to moralize about. But boundaries and edges are not bad as much as they are passing, accidental, sometimes illusory, too often needy of defense and decoration. Our skin is not bad; it's just not our soul. We remain on the circumference of our soul for so long it seems like life. Not many people are telling us there is anything more.

Let's presume there was an earlier age when people had easy and natural access to their soul. I am not sure if this age ever existed, any more than the Garden of Eden, where all was naked and in harmony; but if it did, it consisted of people who were either loved very well at their center or who suffered very much on their surface—probably both. The rest of us have to rediscover and return to the Garden by an arduous route. This movement *back* to paradise is the blood, guts and history of the whole Bible. It is both an awakening and a quieting, a passion for and a surrendering to, a caring and a not caring. It is both center and circumference, and we are not in charge of either one. But we have to begin somewhere. For most of us the beginning point is on the edges. Yet we cannot stay there! The movement beyond is called conversion, integration or holiness.

10

The Unbalanced Male

I was watching *Phil Donahue* one day, and he was interviewing a group of men who were encouraging one another to get in touch with what was deep inside them. The men were well-intentioned—that was obvious—but they just couldn't communicate to Donahue and the audience what they were feeling inside. They just didn't have the skills that we assume women have to intuit what they are feeling and to communicate it. They were unbalanced men, overly developed on the masculine side and underdeveloped on the feminine side. They were trying to correct the balance, but they just couldn't do it in that one hour on television. Their feelings and words were not connected; perhaps they had always deferred to women to do their feeling for them.

Interestingly, some of the women in the audience got angry with these men, calling them wimps and fools for not knowing what they wanted to say. They were laying a male stereotype on the men and criticizing them for not having all the knowledge at their fingertips. Here the men were trying to get in touch with their feminine self, and the women were doing the typically "male" (or shallow masculine) thing of putting them down for not succeeding. How ironic! The incident showed me how men can be—and so often are—debilitated by the white male system, and also how women unconsciously can—and so often do—buy into that same system. The men on the show hated themselves—and the women— for allowing this. But they consciously knew no alternative.

Our technological society, and especially our business world, does not give men any encouragement for the inner journey of self-discovery and spiritual development. In fact, it does just the opposite. If you are an executive or in business for yourself, you have to spend so much time keeping up and trying to get ahead that you often don't have time for relationships with others, much less for a relationship with yourself or God. If you work the traditional eight-to-five schedule, in an office or a factory, society gives you plenty of distractions, stimulants and narcotics to take your mind off the stress and boredom of routine. And, of course, the world never suggests to you that there might be something else to do, some inner course to take, from which no one will make a profit.

By and large, the Church is no help, either. The western world has turned the Church into another corporation, with corporate headquarters downtown in the bishop's office and with company stores conveniently located all around the city and the suburbs. In the fourth century, when Christians were first permitted to practice their faith openly, they allowed the Church to be molded in the image of the Roman Empire instead of insisting that the gospel of Jesus transform the imperial system. Bishops and priests became the executives and managers of a vast new religious organization.

The gospel, however, is not at all concerned with the organization of the Church. It is concerned with conversion and transformation, both of the individual and of society itself. Scripture scholars have to work hard to piece together fragments of the New Testament to come up with even a vague guess as to how the early Church was organized. But men even in the first century were more comfortable with organization than with the spiritual wisdom of the gospel, and so organization won out. By the fourth century those parts of the Gospel that could be organized were kept in the Church, and what could not be organized was by and large left out.

How can you organize a spiritual journey? You can't. How can you organize self-transformation and conversion? It's impossible. You can give guidance. You can give hints and clues. You can offer advice and encouragement. But you can't organize and control spiritual development precisely because it's a matter of *spirit*, and you can't see or control *spirit*.

So the men who ruled the Church organized what they could see and control. They organized outer behavior through canon law and codes of public morality. The laity were commanded to perform good works such as receiving the sacraments and contributing to the support of the Church, and they were forbidden to commit evil deeds eventually neatly categorized into mortal and venial sins.

For at least seventeen centuries the Church has been dominated by the male drive for organization and control, and it has shown little tolerance for real spiritual development and social transformation. In fact, I am convinced that institutions are inherently threatened by people of inner spiritual authority and maturity. They are not codependent on the system. There have been, to be sure, exceptions to this rule, but they are exceptions precisely because the rule was something else.

What were the exceptions? I'd like to think of the early monastic movement as one of them. As the Church became more organized and more systematized, individuals and then groups of men and women opted out of the system to try to live the gospel in the desert, on mountains and in other places where they could pursue spiritual development without outside interference. Eventually, of course, monastic life itself became organized and systematized, and much of the original monastic charism was lost. But it kept reappearing in periodic attempts to reform the monasteries and return them to their original purpose, and many of these attempts did in fact succeed.

Other exceptions to the domination of the male paradigm in the Church can be seen in veneration of the Blessed Virgin and devotion to the saints. None of this was planned or organized at the beginning; it just happened. People felt a need to get in touch with the feminine in God and in themselves, so they spontaneously went toward those figures who could represent it to them. Perhaps it was a need to balance the external masculine domination of the Church with the feminine in God and in themselves. Unlike the clerically planned liturgy and sacraments, feasts of Mary and the saints were festivals that the people organized and in which they could pour out their feelings. Eventually, these too were given official approval, and with that came a certain amount of organizational control, but popular festivals in honor of our Lady and even of our Lord always contained the elements of spontaneity, affectivity and fertility that gave rise to them.

Some of the exceptions to the almost total dominance of maleness in the Church are even humorous. Clerical dress, for example. Men wear robes and dresses, and the higher up the hierarchy they climb the more ornate the gowns and jewelry they allow themselves to wear. This feminine style of dressing did not begin until the imperialization of the Church in the fourth century, but it has been with us ever since. It's as if unconsciously the male need for balance by the feminine expressed itself in men dressing like women.

Fortunately, this condition in the Church is slowly changing. Not rapidly enough for some, to be sure, and not widely enough to be of much help to laypeople in the Church yet. But the decline of vocations to the priesthood in Europe and America is giving more and more women opportunities for ministry that they were denied in the past. These women are bringing back into the masculine-dominated Church at least some of the genuine femininity that it has lacked for so long. They are on parish councils, on liturgy committees, in pastoral ministry, visiting the sick, giving spiritual direction, educating the young, even teaching in seminaries.

Those who oppose the ministry of women in the Church often think that women want to be priests in order to have power and authority over them. They see the rise of women in the Church as a threat to their own male consciousness. It is that, to be sure, but they also fail to see their own deprivation and victimization by the present Church system. And so they fail to appreciate the gift in what they resist.

Perhaps some day they will feel, as the men on *Phil Donahue* felt but could not express, that they need to integrate their own feminine side. But until individuals walk this journey, they will probably not recognize that institutions must do the same. An unwhole man prefers an unwhole institution in order to feel balanced, even though it is a false balance. In fact, the two are codependent on one another. An unwhole institution needs and keeps unwhole men at immature levels of development to ensure its continued existence.

After sixteen years of giving clergy retreats throughout the world, I believe the evidence is overwhelming. The world for sure, but even the Church, is terribly afraid of wholeness.

The sexual polarities are the first fascinations and the final taboos. People who are enlightened on issues of race, war and poverty will often hold out until the end on issues of gender and sexism. We are dealing with deep archetypes here, and our unconscious knows that if we tamper with them we are tampering with almost everything. We will probably not move too quickly here because the stakes are very high and very important. It is a narrow and treacherous path that walks between sexuality and spirituality. But there is no alternative for human beings, and even the Church cannot keep us from this holy marriage.

11

Father Hunger

"Do you see now that fathers
who cannot love their sons
have sons who cannot love?
It was not your fault
and it was not mine. I needed
your love but I recovered without it.
Now I no longer need anything."
—Richard Shelton[15]

Much of the human race experiences an immense father
hunger. It is felt by women, but much, much more by
men. In all my years in the priesthood, working in
community, leading retreats and giving talks around the
world, I have found it to be the single most prevalent
wound in the human soul. And one of the most painful.

Once when I was in California giving a series of
talks, a young man in his early twenties came up to
me in the speaker's lounge and pleaded to talk to
me. I invited him to my room and when we got there,

---

[15]Shelton, Richard. "Letter to a Dead Father." *Brother Songs: A Male Anthology of Poetry.* Ed. Jim Perlman. Minneapolis, Minn.: Holy Cow! Press, 1979, p. 21.

he told me his life's story.

Something he said revealed a lot about his father, who was an engineer. Once when the boy had asked him about God, his father told him bluntly, "Mathematics is my god. If you can't prove it, don't talk to me about it. If it's not logical, I don't believe it." His son was just the opposite, a very sensitive young man, and so he grew up with a stranger for a father. He and his father lived in two different worlds, and their worlds never touched. Nothing life-giving ever passed between them.

As he was telling me his story, I could sense the young man was enjoying, even relishing, the experience. Then suddenly, after about an hour, he just stopped and looked at me.

"You're listening to me!" he said in amazement. "My dad never once listened to me, but you're listening to me! I feel like I love you!"

We had been really close in that hour, probably closer than that boy had ever been to a man, but I had to leave soon to give another talk. So I prayed with him, holding his hands in mine, for a while longer. Finally, I got up and placed my hands on his head in blessing. "I've got to go now."

"I don't want you to leave," he said desperately.

"But I have to give another talk in a few minutes. Why don't you want me to go?"

"When you touched me, it felt so good." Then, worried that his words might be misinterpreted, he added, "I'm not gay or anything, but I felt good when you touched me. My father never touched me, or listened to me. Can I come back again?"

The next day, we met again and the same thing

happened all over. He needed someone to tell his feelings to, someone to know who he was, someone to understand the hurt he felt. He needed someone to affirm and approve him. He needed a father.

Whenever I think about that young man, I realize that he is legion. Thousands and thousands of men, young and old, feel as he does. They grew up without a man's love, without a father's understanding and affirmation. So they always hunger for it, and they search for it from teachers and coaches, ministers and scoutmasters, and anyone who will offer it to them. Later, in the military or the business world, they seek to be approved by their superiors in exactly the same way. They become the good team players, the good soldiers, like Oliver North, who would do anything for the president so long as it met with his approval. They are the best players in the white male system.

I meet father hunger in many different settings. Currently, for example, I am a chaplain in the Albuquerque jail, which is a very macho Hispanic subculture all its own. Whenever the prisoners interact with one another or with the guards, they put on a great display of machismo with all the usual cursing and swearing and acting tough. But whenever one of them is alone with me, the whole picture changes. They are little boys anxious to please me, and I am "Padrecito."

I can remember one man who came to see me. He was well built, and he had a tatoo of Our Lady of Guadalupe on one arm and a naked lady on the other. "Look, Father, I can make her move," he said, flexing his muscle. In his eyes I saw a little boy, trying to get daddy's attention.

Many times prisoners will make excuses just to be alone with me and talk with me. They will ask to go to confession even though, being in jail, they had done little to confess. But they bring up anything, hoping it is a big enough sin, just so they could tell me about their inner lives and their private selves.

After hearing a prisoner's confession, I always lay my hand on his head or shoulder as I give him my blessing. Invariably, if I touch him, he cries. He hangs his head down so I won't see the tears in his eyes, but there he is, sobbing like a little boy needing to be held and hugged. He would never let me do that, of course. But always, after it is over, he tries to make conversation, just to keep me a while longer.

Yes, father hunger is a great gaping wound that many of us—most of us—carry within us, without realizing it or, at least, without being able to name it. It is a deprivation that we are constantly trying to overcome, a need that we are always seeking to satisfy. We cannot be ourselves, we cannot be our own men, because we need to be someone else's little boys. We need him to like us. The separation from the one who is the same as us (our father) is somehow even more destructive than the separation from the one who is opposite (our mother). If manhood doesn't like me, then I'm forever insecure about my own.

Just how destructive is father hunger? How far could a man go to satisfy the need for approval denied by his father? What might he do to release his suppressed anger, if not against his father directly then against what his father represents to him?

The German psychologist, Alice Miller, wrote a

study about a man who had been abused as a child.[16] His father beat him for every little infraction, real or imaginary. He wouldn't even call his son by name. When he wanted the boy to come to him, he whistled for him, as if the boy were a dog. Hatred seethed within the boy, but he could not vent his anger on his father. He kept it within, nursing it. Then, some time later, the son discovered that his grandfather (of whom he knew little) had been Jewish. His distorted thinking led him to believe that this Jewish blood was the reason for his father's behavior.

The boy's name was Adolph Hitler. You already know the rest of his destructive story.

---

[16] Miller, Alice. *For Your Own Good: Hidden Cruelty in Child Rearing and the Roots of Violence*, pp. 142-197. New York, N.Y.: Farrar, Straus & Giroux, Inc., 1983.

12

The Father Wound

Father hunger is also sometimes called the father wound. Psychologists use that term to highlight the woundedness in a man's psyche that results from not having a father—whether it is because the father has died or left the family, because the father's work keeps him absent from the scene most of the time or because the father keeps himself aloof from involvement with his children. In any event, the result is a deep hurt, a deprivation that leads to a poor sense of one's own center and boundaries, a mind that is disconnected from one's body and emotions, and the passivity of an unlit fire.

When I was giving a retreat in Peru, a sister who ministers in Lima's central prison brought this lesson home to me. She described how, as Mother's Day was approaching during her first year there, the men in the prison kept asking her for Mother's Day cards. She kept bringing boxes and boxes of cards for the prisoners to send to mama, but she never seemed to have enough. So as Father's Day approached, she decided to prepare for the onslaught of requests by buying an entire case of Father's Day cards. But that case, she told me, is still sitting in her office. Not one man asked her for a Father's Day card. She couldn't even give them away.

She realized then—and as she told me this story with tears in her eyes, I realized it too—that most of the men were in jail because they had no fathers. Not that they were orphans, but they had never been fathered. They had never seen themselves as sons of men who admired them, they had never felt a deep secure identity, they had never received that primal enthusiasm that comes from growing up in the company of a father. And so they spent their lives trying to become men in devious and destructive ways. They were insecure men who had to prove that they were *macho*, and they did this by committing acts of lawlessness and violence.

Not having reached the deep masculine within them, they look to other men for assurance and affirmation. Not having found that inner strength which gives them a sense of their own personal stability, they are constantly trying to prove who they are. Whether they engage in *macho* games of physical fitness, sexual prowess or business success, they are trying to show themselves and others that they have made it, that they are really men. But their continuous running from one accomplishment to another only proves that they have not made it and subconsciously they feel their own incompleteness. Not having found their self-worth, they try to prove their value by making money, accumulating the things money can buy and exercising power. But their constant search for earned worth, in fact, betrays their inner sense of worthlessness.

Identifying with only the common masculine necessarily causes sexuality problems because the common masculine is incompletely sexual. Jean Vanier, the founder of more than sixty *L'Arche* communities for the handicapped and retarded in Europe and Canada, once told me that he found very few men who did not suffer from sexual and authority wounds. Almost every man in western society, he claims, suffers from unhealed and unwhole sexuality. This wound bleeds excruciatingly in sexual violence toward women and homophobia toward other men. Psychologists are learning that rape, for example, is caused not by sexual desire but by hatred of the feminine. Men who have not discovered and befriended their own femininity hate the feminine hidden in their shadow, but they project that hatred outward into disdain for weakness and anger against women. Hatred and fear of homosexuals also comes out of unhealed and unintegrated sexuality. At its core, such hatred represents a severe disconnection between men's bodies and men's spirits.

Not having found the deep masculine within themselves, many men also have problems with authority. Not having encountered a man with true inner authority, they experience authority as something necessarily external and somewhat arbitrary. They do not know the spiritual authority gained from competence and responsibility, and so they never even dream of looking for it within themselves. Authority for them is never inner wisdom but usually outer obligation. That is the way they experience authority, so that is the way they exert authority—in an authoritarian manner. In doing so, however, they create problems for themselves and others. They create problems for themselves because imposing their will engenders both obedience and passivity, both compliance and resentment, both surface respect and hidden rage. At the same time, they make authority problematic for those under their authoritarian regime. Having seldom had a positive experience of authority they could trust, most men fear authority, they rebel against it or unduly worship it. We fear what we have never met. And many men feel they have never met a good and wise man. (Only women are virtuous and caring!) Thus, most men perpetuate the very system that keeps them imprisoned—whether they are locked into being subordinates or superiors.

Even though there are no guarantees in life, we can help our own sons by sharing our inner lives with them, our thoughts, feelings, dreams and hurts. One psychologist told me that most boys lose their respect for their fathers by the time they reach sixteen. I suppose it is somewhat normal for adolescents to want to break the parental bond around that age. How healthy or unhealthy the break is, however, depends a lot on the quality and style of our fathering. If we have neglected or bullied our sons in their boyhood, the break will be a rejection of abandonment or a rebellion against authority that may never be healed. But if we have affirmed and challenged them into manhood, and shared our own struggles with them, the break will be a loosening of the parent-child relationship that in time will be rebonded in a man-to-man relationship. It is more important to draw our sons into a process with us than to give them too-neat conclusions.

Our sons are not stupid. If they've received good masculine energy from their dads as they were growing up, they're not going to reject it when they've grown. If they've learned to trust the masculine during their boyhood, they'll be able to trust it in us and find it in themselves during their manhood. They may look for affirmation and models elsewhere—among their peers, their teachers and coaches, their real or fictional heroes—but that is normal. No man can be all men, even to his own son, who has to build his own manhood by incorporating parts of many role models into his own adult self. But no smart son will discard the example that his father gave him if what he received was an honest, loving experience of his father and a healthy sense of himself as a man.

A son needs to believe that his father respects and even admires him. As a boy he wants his daddy to be proud of him, but as he grows toward manhood a father's pride can seem very patronizing to him. What he needs all along is not only parental approval but adult respect and honest admiration. If dad waits till junior's a teenager, it's too late. That honoring of the man in the boy is what invites the boy to join the club of men. That honoring is what lets him know that he is finally his father's equal, that he and the father are one. Sons usually admit that a part of them needs and wants to keep dad on a pedestal forever, they need and want him to be their dad and not a total peer. (I recall the deep disappointment and confusion felt by one young man I knew when his dad got on his knees in front of him and confessed his sexual secrets and irresponsible life-style to him.)

The father wound is so deep and so all-pervasive in so many parts of the world that its healing could well be the most radical social reform conceivable. I am convinced that this distortion lies at the bottom of much crime, militarism, competitive greed and family instability. What can we do to heal this wound? I suggest three ways to struggle toward healing.

First, we must work through the hurts we feel to an adult and forgiving relationship with our fathers and father figures. Second, we must nurture and perhaps seek reparenting of our little boy within, through healing prayer, male relationships and perhaps some inner spiritual work with the help of a counselor or therapist. And, finally, we should dedicate some of our own father energies to reforming destructive patriarchal structures in our society and to nurturing and healing the next generation of men.

13

The Empty Soul

Joseph Morton

Most men grow up with an emptiness inside them. Call it father hunger, call it male deprivation, call it a lack of fathering, it's the same emptiness. When positive masculine energy, an energy that can be trusted and relied upon, is not shared from father to son, it creates a vacuum in the souls of men. And into that vacuum demons pour.

Again, we can say that women too need the love and affection of a father, but the sexual dynamics are different. Girls need a father to approve their acceptability as a female. Boys need a father to find their basic identity as a male and to become comfortable with a male mode of feeling. And the father is the first freely chosen object of affection in a person's life.

The mother is not chosen. She is simply there, from the first moments of our life. We even smell like our mother when we are born, for we came from within her, and she smells like us. When we are nursing, we can find our mother's breast with our eyes closed because we know our mother's smell and we move toward it instinctively. Only after some months do we begin to vaguely realize that our body and our mother's are not one but two.

Still, mother is familiar. She is known, she can be trusted. Some months later again, we discern another who is like mother but who is not she. The other is a stranger, the first stranger in our growing world. The other is our father. The father is the first encounter with not-me. His acceptance or rejection is our first clue as to whether the outer world can be trusted.

We do not have to do anything to win our mother's affection. She usually gives it voluntarily, even without our asking for it. But we need to do something to get our father's attention and to make him smile at us. For some unknown reason, that smile from the stranger is more energizing, more affirming than our mother's constant affection. Perhaps it is because we feel he doesn't have to give it, so when he does, it is ever so much more precious. It is our first experience of election, of being chosen.

I once read a report of a study of children who were raised by their fathers at home while their mothers went off to work. The report referred to them as "superkids" because almost all of them succeeded in childhood and adulthood far above the statistical average. No doubt their success in life was due to a number of factors, not the least of which is that they had parents who were creative and free enough that they could successfully reverse the traditional parenting roles in our society. But I suspect, too, that the father's love, which has a different quality about it than mother's love, had a lot to do with their being "superkids." Positive masculine energy, whether from the father or the mother, has the power to give children great self-confidence and assurance.

Speaking from my own experience, I can truthfully say that one of the reasons I became a priest was that my father always believed in me. Whenever I was tempted to doubt myself, or wonder if I was up to trying something, he told me he was sure that I could do it. I never grew up with great problems of self-doubt that I see in so many young people I've worked with.

Now, in the Catholic community where I grew up, the priest was the closest thing to God we knew. From that perspective, becoming a priest was a little like becoming a movie star or an Olympic athlete. It was simply not for everybody. My dad assured me that if I wanted to become a priest, I could do it—provided that God wanted me to be a priest too, of course. But my dad's confidence in me left no room for doubt of myself.

When a father tells a child that he can do something, he can do it. I don't know why that is, except to say that there is some mysterious energy that passes from the male to his children. It is some sort of creative energy that can make things be when they are not, and without which things cannot come to be. When male energy is absent, creation does not happen, either in the human soul or in the world. Nurturance happens, support and love perhaps, but not that new "creation out of nothing" that is the unique prerogative associated with the masculine side of God.

Without the father's energy, there is a void, an emptiness in the soul which nothing but that kind of energy can fill. I have seen it in too many people, men especially. It is a hollow yearning that feeds on praise incessantly and is never satisfied. It is a black hole that sucks in reward after reward and is never brightened by it. It becomes a nesting place of demons—of self-doubt, fear, mistrust, cynicism and rage. And it becomes the place from which those demons fly out to devour others.

It is no accident that Jesus addressed God as *Abba*, Daddy. Even though God transcends male and female, and it is equally true and necessary to refer to God as Mother as well as Father, I think that Jesus understood from within his own soul the emptiness that many people feel. He knew it would be harder and more necessary for most of humanity to say "Daddy" than "Mama." To believe in father-love is for most of us the greater leap of faith. Many who want to throw out the wonderful and sexually charged word "Father" are, I'm afraid, the last ones who should do it.

A mother's love we know. A mother's love we have. It is the father's love we need. It is the father's love we seek. It is the father's confidence in us that gives us the courage to risk, to let go and to grow. Relating to God as Father and experiencing God's love as also from a man, we can dare to believe the full gospel and not just those parts which have to do with security, consolation and belonging systems. A God who is both Father and Mother frees us for a gospel that is fertile, intimate and universally creative.

14

Three Kinds of Men

There is a passage in the New Testament which is very applicable to what I want to say about different kinds of men and the kind of man that Jesus is calling us to be.

> On another sabbath he went into the synagogue and taught, and there was a man whose right hand was withered. The scribes and Pharisees watched him closely to see if he would cure on the sabbath so that they might discover a reason to accuse him. But he realized their intentions and said to the man with the withered hand, "Come up and stand before us." And he rose and stood there. Then Jesus said to them, "I ask you, is it lawful to do good on the sabbath rather than to do evil, to save life rather than to destroy it?" Looking around at them all, he then said to him, "Stretch out your hand." He did so and his hand was restored. But they became enraged and discussed together what they might do to Jesus. (Luke 6:6-11)

In this story there are three kinds of men. The man with the withered hand is one kind of man, the scribes and Pharisees are another and the man Jesus is a third kind. We can learn a great deal about ourselves by looking at these three kinds of men and asking ourselves where we might be if we were in the story.

The man with the withered hand is typical of so many men in the world today. Notice that it is his *right* hand that is withered. That's the functional hand, the producing hand. This man is an image of those who are incapable of achieving what they desire or accomplishing what they would like to happen.

He is weak. He just happens to be there in the synagogue, sitting somewhere. He doesn't have any initiative or determination. He doesn't ask for anything. He doesn't even ask to be cured, as many do in the healing stories in the Gospels. Instead, Jesus has to call him. And when Jesus does call him, he stands there silently. He does what Jesus tells him to do, but we never hear a word from him the whole time. Even after he is cured, he does not thank Jesus or praise God or tell others about it, which is what happens in many other healing stories.

This man gives the impression that he is passive, that he is reacting to things rather than acting in the face of things. He is not going anywhere with his life, and he doesn't even care that he's not going anywhere.

The description fits all too many men today, not only in our American culture but in much of the world today. Most men do not know how to motivate themselves. If they have any motivation at all, it is some form of money, sex or power. They have no internal motivation, and without the external motivations of money, sex and power they do not know how to choose or make decisions about what they want to do with their lives.

Another way to say this is that most men have no interior spirituality. They need something outside (like a law!) to kick them, to get them going, to offer them security, to promote them, to reward them, to make them happy. Spirituality is a matter of having a source of energy within which is a motivating and directing force for living. The man of spirit, or the spiritual man, if you will, is energized by something beyond money, sex and power.

The incident in Luke's Gospel is often called a healing story, but I myself wonder whether he is really healed. Maybe his hand is working again, but nothing else seems to be working. Those of us who have had experience in the healing ministry of the charismatic movement, or who have witnessed healings through the sacramental Anointing of the Sick, know the importance of psychological and emotional follow-through. If a physical healing is not accompanied by spiritual healing, the physical symptoms of the illness often return. Physical healing is always a call to inner change, a change of heart, a change of direction. After he healed people, Jesus often told them to get up and walk, or to go and sin no more. There is no indication in this story that the man ever does anything like this. In response to Jesus' miraculous intervention, he just stands there.

The scribes and the Pharisees represent another kind of man in the world today. In the story, ironically, they are church people. They take religion seriously, yet they are trying to block the work of God. They are involved with religion, yet they want nothing to do with healing, freedom or the giving of life. They are trapped in their heads, caught up in their moral principles, blinded by their doctrines. They watch from a distance, critically observing what is going on, in order to accuse. They are men of ill will.

They are what we might call "power conservatives," holding on to the position and security that institutional religion gives them. Such men are very different from "value conservatives," or people who hold on to the values of the gospel. Under the guise of religious values, what they are really into is power and control. They are not just in the Catholic Church but in Protestant denominations, too, as well as in Judaism and Islam. They are the ambitious spokespeople of religious power, and they use God as a front for their own needs for control. When they are questioned, as Jesus questions the scribes and Pharisees, they are silent or they put up a smoke screen. They are full of indignation, but they do not betray their true motives to anyone, not even to themselves.

Another thing to notice about these men in the story is that they think and act as a group. They are not individuals but representatives of a sort of groupthink which, in this case, is religiosity. It might also be patriotism or capitalism or some sort of ethnic chauvinism. Whatever it is, it is opposed to individual consciousness and personal conscience. Collectivist thinking is one of the cheapest and most common substitutes for personal growth and mature conscience. The Pharisees represent propriety and social control, a very common form of first-stage morality. True conscience and the risks of integrity are beyond their understanding and usually are a serious threat to them.

Finally, we see the man Jesus. In five short verses this one man enters, teaches, recognizes what others are thinking, commands, questions and calmly acts. He faces his accusers without panic because he knows what they are thinking. He speaks with inner authority when he addresses the other two kinds of men. He is not afraid to confront people or to question the law. He knows what he is about to do and he does it. He doesn't explain. He doesn't take credit. He doesn't ask for recognition. He just does the truth and he bears their silent fury.

When Jesus leaves the scene, he goes off into the hills to pray and, after that, he gathers a community together.

> In those days he departed to the mountain to pray, and he spent the night in prayer to God. When day came, he called his disciples to himself, and from them he chose Twelve, whom he also named apostles. (Luke 6:12-13)

Being in a hostile situation, being face-to-face with people who hate you, takes a heavy toll on a man. Living in a negative environment, whether it is at home or at work, is spiritually draining. Jesus recognizes this, and so he finds a way to brace himself against the negativity and debilitating energy of toxic people.

We must never be afraid to do the same. Much codependency has been called love, by less secure men who do not know how to protect their own boundaries. We will talk about this later as necessary "warrior energy." The wise warrior, Jesus, moves out of the ugly situation created by his accusers and away from the spiritual weakness of the man he helped, in order to gather his own spiritual strength.

He finds it, first of all, in communion with God. But he makes it happen, secondly, by forming a new community around himself. He will teach them that there is a new way of living besides the ways represented by the other two kinds of men. He will show them that there is a new way of understanding what is going on in the world and a new way of acting in the face of power and paralysis.

Jesus understands that we do not think ourselves into a new way of living, but we must live ourselves into a new way of thinking. He forms a healthy community of men as a living alternative to the dysfunctional ways that men usually organize themselves. The Church was intended to be God's "new world order."

15

I and the Father Are One

In the Gospel of John, in speaking about his relationship with God, Jesus emphasizes that he and the Father are one. Jesus repeats this theme again and again as though rejoicing in his relationship as Son to the Father.

As we have seen, the phrase that would characterize most men's parental relationship is, "I and my father are not one." This alienation between sons and fathers is a prominent reason why many men become either weak or power-wielding rather than like Jesus.

The American poet, Robert Bly, believes that this father-son alienation has not always been as intense as it is today. Although we cannot assume that down through the ages all men had happy and wholesome relationships with their fathers, he points to a number of factors which suggest that prior to the Industrial Revolution most men had much closer relationships with their fathers than they have had since.[17]

Before the Industrial Revolution, Bly observes, boys

---

[17]Thompson, Keith. "What Men Really Want: An Interview with Robert Bly," *New Age Journal*, May 1982. I am indebted to Bly for this insight and for many others scattered throughout these pages. This article was seminal for my thinking as I prepared the retreat for men on which this book was based.

commonly grew up in a close working relationship with their fathers. They worked on the family farm or in the family business along with their fathers, learning to be farmers or craftsmen or businessmen and making a real contribution to their family's well-being. From the beginning of their lives, therefore, boys grew up with the understanding that they were part of their father's world and that they were important. They did not have to wonder about their identity because they already had it. And they did not have to earn society's approval later in life because they already had their father's approval.

In the nineteenth century, however, men in great numbers left the farms and went to work in factories, and in the twentieth century more and more men left family businesses to work in the office buildings of large corporations. By and large, their sons had access to neither of these worlds. Thus, during the last century and a half, the majority of boys have had to grow up without close contact with their fathers, and without the assurance that they had a place in the world of men.

The result is what I have already characterized as father hunger, or a deep need for masculine acceptance and approval. But the result, according to Bly, is even more far-reaching than that. In addition to the need for a father figure, boys grow up lacking many of the attitudes and perceptions they almost spontaneously acquire when they mature in the company of men. For lack of a male role model, they are uncomfortable in their own role as men. Not seeing how their fathers relate to their feelings, they are awkward with their own feelings. Not seeing how their fathers relate to other men, they lack independence and self-assurance. They tend to be either very submissive to authority or very resentful of authority because, not having learned early on how to trust and work with their fathers in an ongoing partnership, they do not have a healthy conception of authority.

I myself didn't fully appreciate the impact that this change in the father-son relationship has had on men until I was invited to speak in countries outside the United States. In those parts of Africa that are still largely rural and agricultural, for example, I was profoundly impressed by the way that boys who grow up in their tribal villages carried themselves. They walked and behaved with a kind of self-confidence that I don't see in many grown men in our society. Even in their thirties and forties, most American men are still trying to make it as men, pursuing the tokens of manhood in sex, money and prestige. In pre-industrial Africa, though, boys often move with the self-assurance of men and they do not have to earn their worth as we do.

I found the exact opposite in Jamaica, where the traditional family and way of life were destroyed first by actual slavery and later by economic slavery. In that supposedly tropical paradise, men are forced to leave their families to work as field hands or in resorts where they do not make enough for their families to join them. They have to live in company shacks or run-down apartments with other men, and they can get home to their wives and children in the countryside only once a week or a few times a month. The same is true in South Africa.

In Jamaica, during most of the talk that I was giving, I could hear a general rustling of people talking and moving about in the rather large crowd. Then, when I began to speak about the importance of fathering in families, the noise gave way to dead silence. I could tell that my words had touched these people at a very profound level. I was naming something that they were feeling and acknowledging deep within themselves—a suffering and a longing for fathering. Few of them had grown up with a father at home, a father who could be there when they needed him. All of them had experienced the pain of never having really known their fathers.

Although most men in our own country grow up without a strong presence of a father in their life, I never saw how far absent fatherhood can go in an industrial society until I visited Japan. The Japanese are raised almost entirely by their mothers, even more than we are. Child rearing is considered women's work, something beneath a man's dignity. As a result, young Japanese boys at home grow up in a female-dominated environment, especially in the big cities.

Japanese men do not like to come home for supper with their families. They stay at work in the factory or office long into the evening, to demonstrate their loyalty to the company. Their father figure is the supervisor or boss, so they work very hard and spend long hours to please him. They dare not leave work until after the boss has left, and then they go out to have supper with other men.

On a typical evening in Tokyo, the restaurants are filled with throngs of men getting together to unwind from the pressures of the day, to complain and let off steam and to celebrate whatever successes they've had on the job, instead of going home to be with their wives and children. It seemed so evident to me, as I watched them, that they were playing the roles of father and son to each other—assuring and being affirmed, complimenting and being praised, giving advice and asking for it. What they never gave or received at home, they were seeking in the workplace. This emptiness breeds tremendous needs for conformity and acceptance by other men.

It's true. The men all dress alike, in dark suits, and they all behave the same way. In their craving for masculine energy they do not even go home after supper, but instead they go to the bars to drink saki together, or else they go to the baths to soak and steam with other men. Finally, around ten or eleven at night, they start leaving the city, and the subways are filled with silent and sometimes drunken men, going home to sleep.

Ironically, the typical Japanese man turns his entire paycheck over to his wife. She gives him his allowance to stay out at night after she has taken what the family needs to live on. The woman completely controls what happens at home, and neither the husband nor the children have much say in her world. To my mind, this is a very destructive family arrangement, but it explains a lot about the behavior of the Japanese and their great success in business. It is fueled to a large extent by their absence of fathering at home and their need to find it in the workplace. The reassuring company of other men makes the Japanese business world go 'round!

I shudder to think that our own American society might be headed in the same direction, but already we see signs of it. Business executives ride home to the suburbs late in the evening after their children have gone to bed; they take business trips away from their families for days and weeks at a time. Working men stay overtime or work two jobs in order to earn enough money, and the problem for the children is compounded when both parents must or choose to leave the home to work.

To complicate the problem of the absent father, children often learn to perceive their father through their mother's eyes. Without thinking about it, she tells her children what their father is like through the remarks she makes about him when he is not around. Children grow up believing that their father is lazy ("He never does anything around the house."), incompetent ("We'll have to call the repairman."), stupid ("He'll never know."), unsuccessful ("He doesn't make enough money."), uncaring ("He doesn't have the time.") and so on. When he is actually around they see the man their mother has described to them. All too often, he is the absent disciplinarian ("You just wait until your father gets home!").

Even when the portrait painted is not as negative as this, children can never come to really know their father through what their mother tells them about him. Just as a mother's love can never be known through only being told about it, so also a father's love can never be known except by experiencing it. And we are talking here about so much more than simply love. What we are talking about is the entire range of masculine qualities and energies that can only be known directly, through experience. When the father is absent, therefore, the masculine can never be truly experienced for what it is. Especially in the case of boys, masculinity can never be learned directly. What is learned instead is the masculine through the filter of the feminine.

On every "wild man" retreat I have given, I ask the men to discuss their relationships with their fathers in small groups. Without exception, the feedback from the groups always highlights the same two themes: absence and sadness.

The problem is compounded in the areas of religion and spirituality. Not only is the father unable to give a healthy example because of his absence, but even when he is present he usually cannot model religion or spirituality for his children, especially his sons. One priest friend told me that when he asked men how many could remember their fathers ever praying with them personally, *less than one percent could*! Religion in our culture has become the province of the female, and spirituality has become feminized. American Christianity is much more about belonging and consoling than doing, risking and confronting. Nor can Jesus provide a model for them, for we have become so used to seeing Jesus as God that we never truly see Jesus as a man.

In John 10:30, when we hear Jesus saying, "I and the Father are one," we immediately take it in the doctrinal sense that Jesus is identical with God, completely forgetting that the doctrine of the Holy Trinity came to be formulated more than two centuries after that Gospel was composed. I am not denying that the Son is consubstantial (to use the doctrinal terminology) with the Father in the Trinity, but I am pointing out that the

Jesus of the Gospels is not simply the second Person of the Blessed Trinity but a man as well. He is a man speaking about a man's relationship with the God whom he addresses in the other Gospels as *Abba*, Daddy.

What then is the relationship that the man Jesus is referring to when he says, "The Father and I are one"? I think we can understand it best in terms of that human relationship which we have seen is so sorely lacking in most men today, the relationship of identification with the Father. In reading the Gospels there is no doubt that Jesus identified with his Father: that his mission is the one that he received from the Father, that his power is the Father's power, that his spirit is the Spirit of the Father. In more contemporary terms we could say he knew that he was doing his Father's work and that he got his energy to do it from his Father.

Lacking the intimate and genuine relationship with our own fathers that Jesus had with his, it is extremely difficult—almost impossible—for most of us men to become men like Jesus, to become Jesus men. Our spiritual development as men is stunted by our lack of human development as men. Cut off as we are from a deep and rich experience of having been fathered by our human fathers, we have no idea what it means to be fathered by the *Abba* of Jesus. We take the fatherhood of God in an almost biological sense—in the same sense that we can say that some man I hardly know is my father. I have my father's genes, and he provides for me in some way, and that's the end of it.

Our spiritual growth is a difficult journey, therefore, if we try to grow toward God the Father without first having experienced growing toward our human father.

Without the map of our prior experience with our human father to guide us, our spiritual growth toward God is often a blind journey, one of pure faith. It is my experience that unless people have worked through to an adult (mutual, cocreative, forgiving) relationship with their own parents, they will retain an infantile, fearful and self-protective relationship with God. Unfortunately, this type of relationship is very common in the Church today, and, in fact, even encouraged by its structure.

Catholic theology has always believed that grace can only build on nature. In the early stages of spiritual direction, I usually find that eighty percent of people's operative God image is a combination of their Mother and their Father—for good and for ill.

As these human relationships are healed and matured, we become capable of true union with a God who is both Mother and Father. It takes a lot of faith, waiting and darkness to speak such a full name for God. But what else would faith be?

>>> 16 <<<

The Wild Men of India

I had to go to India to find a culture where the concept of the wild man is generally understood and appreciated. I am not suggesting that all Indian males become wild men in the sense that I have been describing. And I am quite aware that western technology and thinking have made inroads into the traditional Indian culture which are, to some extent, undermining it. But India has for thousands of years understood and appreciated the wild man, and to a large extent it still does.

Indians traditionally divide a man's life into four stages. The first stage is that of the student. When a boy is in early adolescence, he is apprenticed to a guru whose task it is to teach the boys in his care what Indian culture and the Hindu religion teach about life and its mysteries. He teaches them the Indian folkways and the Hindu scriptures, and they learn discipline and self-control through meditation and yoga.

The second stage is that of the householder. When a young man is of an age to marry, his parents arrange his wedding and he settles down to raise a family and occupy himself with business. He might become a farmer, a craftsman or a merchant, or even an intellectual, an administrator or a military officer. Today he might even become a professional in the western sense: a doctor, a lawyer, a teacher, an accountant or so on. He is expected not only to provide for his immediate family but also to play a role in his extended family and to contribute to the well-being of his general community in whatever way his time and talents allow. Traditional Indian culture is both family-oriented and civic-minded.

The third stage is that of the seeker. Whereas we in the west tend to take householding and business as the main focus of life, Indians view it as a merely transitional period leading to what we might mistake as early retirement, for it can begin as soon as the man has provided enough for his family that they can get along without him. Generally, this is when his sons are working and providing an income, having themselves become householders, thus freeing him to go on to the next stage in life. Very often it begins around the time that the first grandchild is born.

The seeker is sometimes referred to as a forest dweller. Not that all seekers go to live in the woods, but they often do go off to be alone. We might think of them as the Hindu equivalent of monks, even though they join no religious order and go to no monastery. They might even continue to live in the family household, but apart from the others and no longer as the decision-maker. After years of having experienced life, they are now in a position to begin to understand it, to look for the big picture, as it were. They read their scriptures, they meditate and they talk with gurus, seeking to understand the meaning of life.

How different this is from the western model of work and retirement! Compared with this eastern view of life, ours is terribly narcissistic and shortsighted. When we get a job or enter a profession, it is our own good which we are looking out for or, at best, the good of our immediate nuclear family. If our brothers and sisters aren't making as much money as we are, so much the worse for them. We don't expect anything from them, so they shouldn't expect anything from us, either, except maybe cards on their birthdays or presents at Christmas. We move away from our grandparents and parents, and that's the last we see of them except for holidays. As for our civic consciousness, we may send a few dollars now and then to some charity or other, but it is a tiny fraction of what we spend—and go into debt for—on ourselves. By and large we don't volunteer our services to anyone who cannot pay for them, unless we are doing it for a business organization or some activity which our children are involved in—just further extensions of our own self-interest.

The western ideal of retirement is equally hedonistic. Forget the kids and the community that gave you a living for so many years and, if you can, move far away from them. You've run in the rat race for so long that now at last you have a chance to stretch out, relax and do absolutely nothing. Alternatively, you may see it as a chance to develop your golf swing, to get into that hobby you always wanted or to fix up the basement now that you have the time to do it yourself. All very important, no doubt, but only from a very narrow perspective. Nothing in those activities accounts for personal growth or concern for others, living the gospel or serving others.

Our culture basically does not promote such values, even though our political and religious leaders continue to give lip service to them. We pay them well to maintain a good cover for the moral and spiritual blindness in our society.

The fourth and final stage of the man's spiritual development in India is that of the wise man. Having sought to comprehend the meaning of life, its mysteries reveal themselves to him in his sixties or seventies. He is now in a position to be a guru himself, not necessarily as a professional teacher of the young, but as a man who can be sought after for wise counsel. He has experienced it all—youth and age, masculinity and femininity, health and sickness, good and evil, society and solitude, wealth and poverty, feast and famine, activity and silence, life and death—and now he can put it all together in a meaningful whole, both for himself and for anyone who seeks his wisdom.

I must sadly confess that I do not see much wisdom like that in America. We culturally expect old people not to be wise but to be crotchety, set in their ways and narrow-minded, and all too often they live up to our expectations of them. Yes, we sometimes nostalgically look back toward a simpler time when grandpa and grandma lived close by and shared their accumulated wisdom with the "young 'uns," but we do not expect that time to return. No civilization has survived without the older generation giving itself to pass on its acquired wisdom to the next generation.

How much longer must we continue to live a truncated, two-stage existence when life in its completeness has much more to offer than that? How much longer must we who are men continue to sacrifice our spiritual growth on the altar of success?

The Creed we recite every Sunday says that Jesus "descended into hell" before he moved into Resurrection. Instead of following the wisdom path of our great teacher, we are encouraged in this life to quickly move toward "heaven." Such quick and pseudosuccess breeds empty and hollow men.

Ronald Reagan, for example, never talked about his alcoholic father. If he refused to grieve and feel the pain of his lost father relationship, he may have achieved external success but paid the price of soul wisdom and real father leadership. He is an image of our country and its male impotence.

We have few guides and surely no encouragement for the "descent into hell." We are a culture of light and have little appreciation for darkness. The Indian wild men know more about our Catholic mystics than we do. Our mystical tradition consistently taught that darkness was a greater teacher than light. The "Church Catholic" has within its storehouse much wisdom for would-be forest dwellers and would-be wise men.

Iron John

Even though the wild man as a masculine archetype has largely disappeared from western culture, we do not have to go back too far in our history to find traces of it. The classic story being used by men's groups today is from *Grimm's Fairy Tales*: the story of Iron John, or Eisenhans, as he is called in German. I have summarized the story below.

◆ ◆ ◆

Once upon a time there lived a king whose castle was right next to a large forest where all sorts of game roamed about. One day he sent a royal hunter into the forest to shoot a deer, but the hunter did not return. "Perhaps he had an accident," thought the king, so the very next day he sent two other hunters into the forest to look for the one who was missing, but they did not come back, either. On the third day he gathered all the royal hunters together and instructed them, "Search the entire forest and do not return until you have found the three missing men." But all these hunters, too, like the first three, never came back. Even the hunting dogs they had taken into the forest were never seen again.

From that day forward, no one dared venture into the forest nor did they see anything moving except for an occasional eagle or hawk flying above. The forest lay completely still and silent.

This state of affairs went on for years, until one day a hunter from a distant land asked the king if he could look for game in the royal forest. Remembering what had happened to the missing men, the king was reluctant to grant the request. He told the hunter, "I am very afraid that if you went into the dangerous forest you would fare no better than the others, and that you would never get out of it alive." To which the hunter replied, "My lord, I do not know the meaning of fear. I will gladly face the danger."

Into the forest strode the hunter with his hound. It was not long before the dog picked up the scent of a deer and barked for the hunter to follow him. Then the dog ran ahead, until he came to the edge of a pool of water that was so deep he hesitated before trying to cross it. Suddenly, a bare arm reached up out of the dark pond, grabbed the hound and pulled him under.

When the hunter saw what had happened, he ran back to the castle and got three men with buckets to empty all the water out of the pond. They worked hard for many hours, and as the dark waters began to be drained away, they beheld a wild man lying on the bottom. His body was covered with hair the color of rusted iron. The hunter and his helpers bound the wild man with ropes and dragged him off to the castle.

The sight of the wild man caused great wonder and

alarm, so the king had him locked in an iron cage in the middle of the courtyard. He forbade anyone under threat of exile to open the door to the cage, and he entrusted the key to no one less than the queen herself. And from then on, anyone could again go safely into the forest.

Now, the king had a son who was eight years old, and one day when the prince was playing in the courtyard with his golden ball, the ball bounced into the iron cage. "Give me back my ball," said the boy. "Not until you open the door for me," answered the wild man. "No," said the boy, "I dare not do that. The king has forbidden it." And with that, he ran away.

The very next day, however, the boy came back and demanded his ball again. Again the wild man said, "Open the door for me." But the boy would not do it.

On the third day, the king went off on a hunt. His son came back yet again, and this time he said, "Even if I wanted to, I could not open the door because I do not have the key." To which the wild man replied, "It is lying under your mother's pillow. You can surely get it." Upon hearing this, the boy threw all care to the wind, for he really wanted his ball, and stole the key.

The young prince returned shortly and unfastened the lock, but as he pulled the heavy door open, it pinched his finger. As soon as the door swung open, the wild man stepped out, gave the boy his golden ball and started to hurry away. But the boy was frightened, and he called after him, "Oh, wild man, if you run away I shall be punished! Please don't run away!" Whereupon the wild man turned around and came back. He picked the boy up, sat him on his shoulders and carried him off into the forest.

♦ ♦ ♦

What are we to make of this tale? Like so many other fables and myths it is really an allegory with a great deal of meaning hidden in it. It is exactly the type of story that depth psychologists frequently analyze by taking the characters and their actions as symbols of what is going on inside a person even though the person may be completely unaware of it. In this particular case, however, the story is not someone's personal dream but a cultural myth that represents something in what Carl Jung and others have called the collective unconscious. From that perspective, it is clearly a tale about the wild man in all of us.

Let us examine the symbolism step-by-step.[18]

At the outset, the king's hunters disappear without a trace. Although he sends others out to look for them, the king never asks the one question that really needs to be asked, namely, what is it that is causing the men to be lost? Like most of us, the king turns away from his problem rather than facing it. In this instance, the problem obviously has something to do with the loss of manpower or manliness. He leaves the forest, which is the part of his life with the problem in it, undisturbed. All appears to be peaceful and quiet, but the danger in fact has not gone away.

The only one with the courage to face the danger is a foreigner who discovers where the cause of the king's problem is hidden. He calls for assistance, and with great

---

[18] I was first led to this analysis by Robert Bly, in the interview cited earlier. His fuller treatment of the tale and its implications for today can be found in *Iron John: A Book About Men* (Addison-Wesley, 1990).

labor he and the others empty out the water from the deep pond. The stranger represents a certain willingness to look into the problem area, but the king himself at the same time represents continued resistance to the idea. The men with buckets dip into the dark pool of the unconscious, but it is only with great effort that they uncover this mysterious region in order to get to the bottom of things.

What they find is a big, hairy, naked man. They tie him up and bring him back to the castle, where the people are fascinated by the wild man's brute energy. The king does not know what to do with this uncontrolled and frightening strength, however, so he locks the wild man up where he can do no harm. With that, the king returns to his old pursuits, as though nothing at all has happened. Very symbolically, though, the queen holds the key to the wild man's cage, for the woman has the power to unlock his energy or, as in this case, to keep it locked up.

Next on the scene comes the young prince. He is eight years old, what used to be called the "age of reason," when children emerge from unreflective innocence and begin thinking. He is also playing with a golden ball, which in mythology often represents wholeness. So the boy in his innocence comes face-to-face with his father's wild man—who, because the boy is the king's son, is also his own wild man. The boy wants his wholeness, but the only way he can get it is to let the wild man out.

Iron John tells him that the key to it all is under the queen's pillow for, as we have seen, the way to the wild man is through the feminine. The boy is afraid of what might happen to him if he lets out the wild man, but his desire for wholeness prompts him to sneak into his mother's bedroom anyway to steal the key.

What are we to make of this? I myself take it to symbolize the ambiguity of the feminine in most of our lives. On the one hand, the wild man locked inside us is telling us that his incredible strength can be reached by moving into the space of the feminine, yet so often the woman who could lead us into that space wants to prevent us from getting in touch with the wild man. Rebekah so rejected her hairy, hunter son, Esau, that she betrayed him in favor of the gentle Jacob (see Genesis 27). This is not a new issue.

In my own life, I have to admit, that woman is my mother. Right from the very beginning of my ministry, whenever my mother would hear about me getting into strange things like charismatic Masses or war protests, she would call me up and chide me for trying to be different. Why can't I just be the nice, docile priest she had wanted her son to be, she always wants to know. It is very hard to resist those maternal voices that do not understand or support risk taking.

I often see the same in other priests' lives, not just in reference to their mothers but in reference to "our holy mother, the Church," as we used to say. Holy mother doesn't want her sons to be different, she does not want them to do anything that might rock the boat or tarnish the family image, even if they are doing it to promote the gospel—which is what the Church is supposed to be all about. In most male puberty rites the young boy must separate from his mother. If you think this is strange or unnecessary, witness Jesus' action at age thirteen in the temple (Luke 3:41-52).

We can imagine the boy's trepidation as he returns from the queen's bedroom with the key. Will the wild man eat him? Will he be punished by his well-meaning, but possessive parents? Overcoming his doubts, the boy swings open the heavy door, suffering a small hurt as he does this. The wild man never emerges without pain, yet it is never as great as we might have feared.

Once the wild man is let out, he is surprisingly gentle. He does not devour the boy and he gives him back his ball, as he had promised. Then, when the wild man begins to run off, the boy begins to fear his parents again, so the wild man returns and carries the boy off on his shoulders.

In the final scene, the boy—the innocent, inquiring yet brave boy in each of us—has befriended the wild man, whose mighty energy now carries him off. To where? The forest. But what lies in the forest? The tale ends ambiguously.

Should we think that the boy becomes a wild man like Iron John, lurking in a muddy pool to devour unwary passersby? I prefer to think that the pair, now united, are different from what each of them was separately. The boy seated on his shoulders has become the wild man's eyes and vision, and the wild man has become the boy's masculine energy—the energy his father never gave him.

Together they go off to adventure in the forest—and probably beyond.

$$\blacktriangleright\blacktriangleright\blacktriangleright \ 18 \ \blacktriangleleft\blacktriangleleft\blacktriangleleft$$

Accomplishment and Community

"You may be 38 years old, as I happen to be. And one day, some great opportunity stands before you and calls you to stand up for some great principle, some great issue, some great cause. And you refuse to do it because you are afraid.... You refuse to do it because you want to live longer.... You're afraid that you will lose your job, or you are afraid that you will be criticized or that you will lose your popularity, or you're afraid that somebody will stab you, or shoot at you or bomb your house; so you refuse to take the stand. Well you may go on and live until you are 90, but you're just as dead at 38 as you would be at 90. And the cessation of breathing in your life is but the belated announcement of an earlier death of the spirit."

—Martin Luther King, Jr.[19]

---

[19]Martin Luther King, Jr., "But, If Not." Sermon, Ebeneezer Baptist Church, November 5, 1968. Copyright ©Martin Luther King, Jr., Estate, 1968.

Again, I remind the reader that I use the terms masculine and feminine to describe the two polarities that are actually found within the same person. I retain the "sexually-charged" words precisely because they have so much power to evoke and enlighten. If they bother you because they appear to be limiting or attributing too much to sexuality, you may think of the ancient Chinese terms yin and yang, or physical terms such as hot and cold, or electrical terms such as positive and negative charges. But all of these terms are still less revealing, in my opinion, than those powerful words— masculine and feminine. We are delving into the depths of personal power here; that is probably why the feelings about how we identify these energies run so deep.

Hence, we can say that masculine energy is resolute, decisive and outgoing. It is oriented toward work, task and accomplishment. Men who overidentify with their masculine sides can become workaholics, so involved with the world of things that they have no time for the world of personal relationships. Their wives and children suffer from their inability to be concerned with their families in any more than a material and financial way. They see themselves as good providers, but they are so concerned with economic well-being that they never think about their families' emotional well-being.

Feminine energy, on the other hand, is oriented toward the inner, toward union, toward relationship. It is attuned to feelings and connections. It is usually concerned with people before principles. It is often more concerned with the primary family than the larger world.

All too often, however, the ultimate focus of a man's outwardly directed energies is the home—not the home as family but the home as house. He makes money in order to buy a nice house in a good neighborhood, and then he makes more money in order to buy a better house or to fix up the one that he's settled in for a while. He moves from starter home to family residence to vacation house and finally to a place for retirement. All his life, paradoxically, he is engaged in what one would expect to be a typically feminine pursuit—fixing up the house. The unconscious motivation for his doing this is that he is giving in to the demands of the shallow feminine, his unrecognized need for a warm, safe, protected environment.

The ancient Greeks in one respect were far more balanced than modern men. The ideal Greek man was accomplishment-oriented. His focus was not on his house, however, but rather on the city-state in which he was a citizen. He was expected to be a warrior in his youth and a businessman in his middle years, but he was supposed to direct his energies toward the betterment of his community. All through his life, moreover, he was expected to engage in politics and be concerned for affairs of state. A man who did not was called *idios*, self-centered.

What today we call an *idiot*, therefore, was originally a man who did not balance his masculine and feminine energies in the world of manly accomplishment. Not having integrated his outward and inward concerns in the social sphere, he divided his life between the public world of action and the private world of his personal concerns. From the Greek perspective, this life-style was idiocy, yet for Americans this is normal. Few men in our society concern themselves with what is going on in the world around them except insofar as it affects their private interests. Few Americans worry how their business decisions impact on the larger society.

In the Renaissance the Greek ideal of balanced masculine and feminine energy found expression in the layout and architecture of European cities. Private wealth and public funds combined to create buildings and spaces that benefited the entire community. Churches and civic centers, plazas and promenades, fountains and statues, parks and gardens made cities livable and enjoyable for everyone. Community-mindedness balanced private interest.

Moreover, in New Mexico, where I now live, the Pueblo Indians have a strong sense of community, as can be seen in their dances and their common work projects. Interestingly enough, in the Pueblo culture there is almost a bias *against* fixing up one's private dwelling too much. If any decoration is done on an individual dwelling, it is done only on the inside. The Pueblos are anxious to let the outside look plain and like everybody else's, even ramshackle by our Anglo standards.

Contrast this philosophy with the typical American focus on house and neighborhood that shows little concern for larger social issues. Cities deteriorate because the affluent move to the suburbs, and then suburbs deteriorate when the wealthy want to reclaim the cities. Neighborhoods protect themselves from the "wrong kind of people"—Blacks or Hispanics, the retarded or the handicapped—moving in and "lowering property values." Masculine energy fails to move beyond its own backyard and get involved with the social good. Unconsciously dominated by the shallow feminine, men become emasculated citizens.

This is why the feminist movement has much to offer our world and culture. It can show us the dark and destructive side of patriarchy ("the rule of the fathers"). An integrated and maturing male has nothing to fear and everything to gain from healthy feminism, especially when it is based in faith and wisdom drawn from the energies of the deep feminine, and is not an end in itself (a desire to substitute the rule of men with the rule of women).

Balanced masculinity shows itself in *action undertaken for the sake of others*. The integration of male and female energies leads to accomplishments that result in the good of the community. There is a balance of action and compassion which combines the desire for doing with a sensitivity for the needs of others.

Without such a balance, the unbridled use of masculine energy destroys the very world in which it operates. It exalts the individual at the expense of the community, and it promotes private interest to the detriment of the public good. Ultimately it can even undermine the family that it wants to preserve and protect, for it has no sense of relationship, and a family is not an isolated unit but a relationship within a larger social fabric of relationships.

≫ **19** ≪

The Yin and the Yang of Things: Feminine and Masculine Virtues

If I were to give a name to the virtues that I was taught in the seminary, I'd be sorely tempted to call them something like company virtues. They're the kinds of qualities that people at the top like to instill in people on the bottom so that they don't rock the boat and they keep the company's business running smoothly.

In one sense they can also be called feminine virtues because the great feminine strength is building and maintaining relationships, which traditionally has meant keeping the family together. We have already seen that feminine energy moves toward the center, and women in many societies including our own can be credited with maintaining the center, holding the family together, even when the rest of the world may be crumbling around them.

This is undoubtedly a task that needs to be performed in any group or organization, but when that is the whole company business, when that is all that the leadership in the Church is interested in, for example, then something is sorely lacking. What is lacking is masculine virtue, the strengths of the scout and the journeyman, who always venture out, beyond, to the new frontier instead of endlessly protecting the old boundaries.

What I am calling the feminine virtues are humility, obedience, openness, receptivity, trust, forgiveness, patience and long-suffering. They are the sort of virtues which appear soft, naive and even dangerous to men in business, politics or the military. Yet, strange to say, in the totally male subculture of the Catholic clergy, they were also the virtues that were drilled into all the new trainees—which is why we can also think of them as company virtues. They are the kinds of qualities that a king wants all his subjects to have. If they do, his role is a lot easier.

I am not denying that these are virtues. They are great strengths of character, and one does not acquire them easily. What I am pointing out is that these are strengths needed for holding the family, the company or the Church together. In and of themselves, however, they have no power to move in any outward direction. Being focused on the group, they harness no energy to move the group forward. For that, what is needed is an entirely different set of strengths or virtues.

Some of the virtues that I would place in this category are self-possession, leadership, truthfulness, decisiveness, responsibility, closure, intelligence, inner authority, challenge, courage and risk taking. We have never heard very much about virtues such as these. Many of the saints had these virtues, but that is why they were usually canonized several centuries later, after the dust had settled and they could be domesticated.

By *self-possession* I mean the ability to be in touch with

your clear center, your feelings and your motives. A self-possessed man is one who knows what his values are and acts on them. He has self-knowledge, self-awareness. He knows where he's coming from, and he acts on the basis of freely chosen values rather than reacting to situations or to demands that other people place on him. He is his own man, he hasn't been bought. He isn't trying to please people. He is just trying to do what he believes in his own heart is right. He seeks the will of God, even against his self-interest.

One down-to-earth example of this is something that I saw people doing in the New Jerusalem community. In recent years many of them came to the realization that they were caught up in a consumerism that continually spiraled upward—the more they made, the more they spent on themselves. They felt that it was not right for them to keep buying more luxuries, especially when there were so many other people in the world, in Cincinnati and even in their own neighborhood who did not have the necessities of life. So husbands and wives sat down together, figured out what their families *needed* to live on and decided to give the rest away. They planned to give it away, and they followed through on their plans—unlike most people, for whom charity is what they give if there is any money left over from spending on themselves.

A good example of the opposite is something that M. Scott Peck talks about in *People of the Lie*.[20] At one point in that book he talks about the people who live and work in corporate America, never doing what they

---

[20]Peck, M. Scott. *People of the Lie: The Hope for Healing Human Evil*. New York, N.Y.: Simon and Schuster, 1983.

believe is right because they do not even know what they themselves believe in. They have been told early in life what success means, and they live their entire lives living up to society's definition of success. They make friends only with the right kind of people because that is the way to promotion and success. They marry the right kind of wife, live in the right kind of neighborhood in the right kind of house with the right kind of dog, drive the right kind of car and have the right number of children. But the "right" thing is never something that they themselves deeply believe in. If the "right" thing to do were changed tomorrow, they would change what they do just as quickly as they change makes of automobiles and styles of clothing. Instead of being self-possessed, they are possessed.

If self-possession is the virtue of self-knowledge, then *truthfulness* is the virtue of reality knowledge. It is the ability to see clearly what is going on in the world, or in the situation around you, and to name it for what it really is. This virtue is admittedly difficult to acquire because it presupposes that you have a good deal of objectivity and detachment from the situation you are judging and that you have adequate knowledge for making a balanced judgment. We are always inclined to project our own feelings and attitudes onto other people and to let our personal biases and prejudices skew our perceptions of reality. This virtue assumes that you can step out of yourself, as it were, and instead of looking at something from your own point of view, look at it from another perspective. It assumes that you are willing to put in the time and make the effort to reach the truth and also that you are willing to admit when you have made a mistake.

Here at the center in Albuquerque, we call it the development of "the third eye," the objective self-observer.

The truthful man is therefore one who is concerned with finding out the truth, no matter what it costs him. He wants to get to the bottom of things. He is not satisfied with first impressions. He is able to set aside his own self-interest and to seek the truth for the good of all concerned. What he wants to know is not what will benefit himself alone but what is objectively right and fair.

I see an example of this kind of truthfulness in Pope John Paul II's encyclical, *On Social Concern*. To write that document the pope obviously gathered information from all over the world before setting pen to paper, and he reflected on what he had learned in the light of objective gospel values. Though he himself is a man of considerable power with access to great wealth, he was able to look at world economics from the viewpoint of the poor and the powerless. In reaching his conclusions he did not hold himself back from condemning the evils of both communism and capitalism.

The counterexample can be seen in those who objected to the encyclical from their own privileged positions of affluence and influence, especially in our own country. Many of these are "power conservatives" who are willing to praise the pope when he takes stands on individual morality but who are unable to be objective in matters of social morality. Since their own self-interest is identified with business and profit, they cannot identify with the legitimate needs and rights of the poor. They criticize the pope for mixing religion and economics, when what he is doing is showing the objective implications of the gospel for the way that people should treat one another. At the same time, they are blind to the way that they mix religion and economics by assuming that God blesses the concentration of wealth in the hands of a few, the so-called "prosperity gospel."

Responsibility is my way of talking about the opposite of passivity. Catholics have been told all their lives to be obedient, but this has bred an enormous amount of passivity in their souls, and it needs to be counterbalanced by something like responsibility. Call it initiative, if you like, but what I am talking about is the ability to size up a situation, see what has to be done and do it. A responsible man does not need to be told what to do; he simply does it and takes responsibility for it. He makes the difference between needs being met and people having to do without until someone higher up gets around to recognizing the need. If he needs help, he gets it. If he needs someone else's authorization, he gets it. But the simple fact that he doesn't have someone around him or above him to tell him what to do does not prevent him from taking the initiative and bearing the consequences, both good and bad.

Again, I have seen examples of this in New Jerusalem, probably because it is a community run by laypeople. If the people in the community don't do it, it doesn't get done. They can't go to the pastor or the bishop and ask him to do something for them. On the other hand, if people in the community want to do something, the pastoral team generally looks it over and gives it their blessing. When the American bishops came out with their pastoral letter, *The Challenge of Peace*, some of those who believed the document addressed important social and moral issues organized into teams that made presentations in Cincinnati parishes. When children in the New Jerusalem community started to be of an age that they needed religious instruction, their parents reviewed the possibilities, decided on a program and got the help they needed to run it every week.

Closure is another name for decisionmaking. It is the strength needed to make a decision when a decision has to be made, to let the chips fall where they may and, if necessary, pick up the pieces. Closure is needed to balance the feminine virtue of openness, which implies a willingness to listen to everyone concerned. The balanced male has that openness, but he is also able and willing to make decisions. He is not always popular, and I am not even suggesting that he is always right. But a lot of times we cannot find out that a decision is the wrong one until after it is made. The man of closure is, therefore, not afraid of being disliked, not afraid of making mistakes and is willing to learn from them.

Closure is the virtue that many of the young fathers in the New Jerusalem community seemed to be lacking when we began to suspect that men needed something more than the development of the feminine virtues of openness, acceptance and caring. Children would be arguing, and the fathers had no skills for taking the matter in hand and settling the argument. Children would want things, and the fathers didn't know how to give them a clear yes or no. Children would be stubborn, and the fathers were helpless. Children would be undisciplined, and the fathers did not know how to discipline them. The fathers were afraid of being unpopular with their own children, but in the end they did not please anyone. They, perhaps, did not know their own boundaries or lacked the fortitude to defend them.

Tolerance and openness are virtues in the life of one with clear authority; they are sad excuses in the lives of those afraid of their own authority. Many modern, liberal types are not really open; they just don't believe in anything strong enough to fight for it.

By *challenge* I mean what today is sometimes called tough love. If forgiveness is the ability to let go of hurts, challenge is the ability to risk hurting. A man who is able to challenge does not close his eyes to what is going on, but he confronts it. He does not do this in negative or destructive ways but in ways that help people to change their behavior. Very often this takes real skill, besides strength of character.

Another name for challenge is forthrightness. It is the ability to call a spade a spade and to not beat around the bush. It means being able to say, with Jesus, "I forgive you," but then to add, as he often did, "Go and sin no more." Challenge means being willing to risk argument, misunderstanding and disagreement. It means being willing to stick your neck out for a person or a value which you believe in.

The need for challenge can be seen in almost every area of life where something needs to be corrected. A man who has children who are not doing well in school does not help them if he doesn't face the problem and creatively challenge them to do better. If he suspects that they are being tempted into drugs or premarital sex, he needs to let them know that he is aware of it, what his values are and where he draws the line. If he has an alcoholic wife, he needs to understand the destructiveness of codependence and learn to support his wife without supporting her habit. If he works in a place where something unethical is happening, he needs to be able to name that and to stand up for what he knows is right. If he lives in a society that condones immorality and injustice, he needs to devote some time and energy to challenging it. By sitting back and thinking that the problem will go away, he does no good for himself, his family or his country.

Self-possession, truthfulness, responsibility, closure and challenge are some of the virtues I am naming masculine. These are some of the more fundamental ones. They illustrate what manly virtue is all about and what place virtue has in a man's life.

The world of nature gives us a good image of manly virtue in the way that eagles teach their young to fly. Eagles build their nests on high cliffs, and like all birds they care for their young until it's time for them to leave the nest. Now, I've seen young sparrows and robins who seem to know when it's time to get out of the nest. When their muscles are strong enough and their feathers are long enough, they just flap their wings and off they go. But eaglets are not like that. Maybe it's because it seems such a long way down from the cliff, or maybe it's because they just want to keep eating off mom and dad, but they actually have to be pushed out of the nest. So at a certain point the father eagle knows the time has come, he pushes one out, and it falls screaming and squawking toward the ground below. He flies down beside it, and just before the eaglet crashes he dives toward the scared youngster, catches it in his powerful grip and brings it back up to the nest. But if the eaglet hasn't learned to fly, the father sends it through the whole routine again. That is a good image of masculine energy: being self-possessed, recognizing the objective reality, taking responsibility, making a decision and challenging to growth.

Nothing I have said, however, implies that women cannot have this type of energy or that they should not possess these virtues. A woman who has developed her masculine side will have these strengths and they will make her a more dynamic and integrated person. We are not talking here about either/or but about both/and. We are always talking about complementarity of opposing energies within the whole person. We are talking about a healthy androgyny.

I am told that mother eagles give flying lessons just as well as father eagles.

20

Left Brain and Right Brain

In recent years a great amount of research has been done on the human brain. Some of the most interesting findings have dealt with the different functions of the two brains' hemispheres.[21]

Physiologists have known for a long time that the right and left sides of the *cerebrum* (the large mass of brain tissue that composes five-sixths of the human brain) are almost completely separate, mirror images of one another. With regard to body functions, the left side sends and receives messages to the right side of the body, and vice versa. What we see to the left of us, for example, registers in the right side of our brain. When we extend our right arm to shake hands, the left brain has sent the signal.

The two hemispheres are connected at one point by what is called the *corpus callosum*, a bundle of nerve fibers that acts as a bridge across which the

---

[21]A good, readable summary is *Left Brain, Right Brain* by Sally Springer and Georg Deutsch (W. H. Freeman, 1985). To more fully appreciate the importance of right-brain thinking, read Thomas R. Blakeslee, *The Right Brain: A New Understanding of the Unconscious Mind and Its Creative Powers* (Doubleday, 1980).

hemispheres communicate with one another. When we look through both eyes, for example, input is shared across this bridge. When we move both arms, the movement is coordinated to some extent through these nerve fibers.

The more recent discoveries by psychologists have to do with functions that originate in the brain, such as thinking, feeling and talking. Rational, logical and thinking functions tend to be located in the left hemisphere. Creative, intuitive and feeling functions tend to be located in the right hemisphere. Both sides of the brain make important contributions to human intelligence, but in any given person, one side tends to dominate. As it turns out, more men are left-brain dominant, whereas more women are right-brain dominant, although all of Western civilization is strongly left-brain, even most women.

These findings have important implications for what we have been saying about masculinity, femininity and androgyny. One such implication is that there appears to be some physiological basis for typically masculine and typically feminine modes of behavior. In wanting to be logical and orderly in their approach to things, and in preferring to analyze and judge, men tend to use their left brain more. In wanting to be relational and harmonious in their approach to people, and in preferring to accept and connect, women tend to use their right brain more.

Another implication has to do with the psychology of knowledge. Conceptual and analytical knowledge is largely a left brain function, whereas experiential knowledge and seeing the relations between things and how they affect people are for the most part right brain functions. To understand anything really well, we have to use both sides of our brain. Specialists who know a lot of theory but who "have their head in the clouds" and "never come down to earth" can be too heavily dependent on left brain thinking. Other people who have no use for book knowledge and who base all their decisions on feeling and intuition can be relying too much on right brain thinking. Full human knowledge is always integrated and wholistic.

The truly wise person is a wholistic person, and the well-integrated personality is an androgynous personality. Each side of the total person has its own gifts to bring to the total personality. If either side is too dominant, what results is a lopsided, compulsive personality.

Many men do great harm to themselves and the people around them by overidentifying with their left brain, masculine side. They rely so heavily on their version of reason and logic that this gift becomes a compulsion. They follow their ideas so blindly that they walk all over people. They are so taken up with the outer world of things that they leave no room for the inner world of relationship and intuition. They so glorify left brain intelligence that it becomes their god—a god which is really a demon in disguise because it falsifies reality. Looking at the world through the left brain alone makes a part of reality look like the whole of reality.

Depth psychology gives men yet another reason for discovering and developing their intuitive and sensitive side. Carl Jung calls the unrecognized side of a personality its *shadow*. Besides the part of our self which we are consciously aware of, there is also a part lurking in the darkness of our unconscious. For most women, it is their hidden masculine abilities, and for most men, it is their hidden feminine abilities. Even though we are not aware of it, both sides of our brains are always active, both sides are always at work in us. When we are consciously looking at the world through one of the sides, we are unconsciously reacting to it through the other side as well.

Men who overidentify with the masculine in them leave the feminine shadow in darkness. A man's feminine shadow can also be projected onto women, whom they are either infatuated with or whom they look down upon as weak and vulnerable. When they fail to integrate their own deep feminine side, men often act out of an occasional awkward state that is feminity at its worst: pettiness, deceitfulness, cheap vanity, manipulation, sarcasm and so on.

If a man's feminine side is not only undeveloped but also repressed, it shows up as fear of femininity, uncomfortableness with women and even hatred of homosexuals. Ironically but understandably, the *macho* man has doubts about his own masculinity and so he is driven to constantly prove it to himself and others. His anxiety comes out of his own repressed and unrecognized femininity, for his unconscious mind is suggesting to him that he is not aware of who he really is.

For a man to develop spiritually, he needs to tune into what is going on in the right side of his brain. Spiritual insight and intuition come mostly through the right brain, so to recognize and understand what is going

on inside himself, he needs to find ways to raise his
right-brain consciousness.

One of the best ways to do this is by paying attention
to dreams. As soon as we go to sleep, the left brain shuts
down for the night and the right brain takes over. By
trying to remember dreams and learning how to
interpret them, we can greatly develop our spiritual
self-awareness. This book is not the place to discuss the
symbolism of dreams or the techniques of dream
analysis, but those who are interested in this avenue of
spiritual development can find many good books on the
subject and even courses on dream interpretation.[22]

Another helpful technique for getting in touch with
the right brain and allowing it to operate more freely is
spiritual journaling. Keeping a spiritual journal is not the
same as keeping a diary in which one lists the external
events of the day, but rather it is a technique of writing
every day in such a way as to allow the unconscious to
come to the surface and unexpressed thoughts to be
verbalized. Again, this book is not the place to discuss
such techniques, but good books and workshops are
available to help those interested to develop this method
of getting in touch with their feminine side.[23]

In general we need to open up the non-rational right

---

[22]For example, Ann Faraday, *Dream Power* (Berkley Publishing Group, 1986);
Morton Kelsey, *Dreams: A Way to Listen to God* (Paulist Press, 1978); Louis
Savary, Patricia Burns and Strephon Kaplan Williams, *Dreams and Spiritual
Growth: A Christian Approach to Dreamwork* (Paulist Press, 1984); Richard J.
Sweeney, *Understanding Your Dreams* (audiocassettes, St. Anthony
Messenger Press, 1991).

[23]The most thorough and complete book is still the one by Ira Progoff, *At a
Journal Workshop: The Basic Text and Guide for Using the Intensive Journal
Process* (Dialogue House, 1977). A bit more readable is Tristine Rainer, *The
New Diary: How to Use a Journal for Self-Guidance and Expanded Creativity*
(J. P. Tarcher, 1979).

brain by all those skills that often seemed lightweight, unnecessary or even superfluous: art, music, poetry, drama, dance, prayer, ritual, symbolism, literature, leisure and silence. If we are still avoiding these, we are not only avoiding our own vast unconscious, but we are likely avoiding the depths of God's Spirit.

21

A Masculine Magnificat

The Magnificat

And Mary said: "My soul proclaims the greatness of the Lord and my spirit *exults in God my saviour;* because *he has looked upon his lowly handmaid.* Yes, from this day forward all generations will call me blessed, for the Almighty has done great things for me. *Holy is his name,* and *his mercy reaches from age to age for those who fear him.* He has shown the power of his arm, he has routed the proud of heart. *He has pulled down princes* from their thrones *and exalted the lowly. The hungry he has filled with good things,* the rich sent empty away. *He has come to the help of Israel his servant, mindful of his mercy*—according to the promise he made to our ancestors—of his mercy to Abraham and to his descendants for ever."

Mary stayed with Elizabeth about three
months and then went back home.
                                        —Luke 1:46-55

Recently I was asked to interpret Luke 1:39-56 from the
perspective of a masculine spirituality. A German group
is publishing a study of this classic Marian text from
different viewpoints to clarify the various assumptions
and biases that each group "suffers" under. Hopefully
the fundamentalist, the feminist, the historical-critical
and the masculine will all have something to offer one
another. When we allow others their bias, we are more
likely to see and recognize our own. Each has limitations
and each has a great truth. To work with both is to enter
into Scripture in a way that is both faith-filled,
demanding and always open to God's transcendent
Word.

A *hermeneutic* is the grid by which and through
which a Scripture scholar interprets a text. A good
scholar is honest and consistent about his hermeneutic.
She tells you exactly why and how she can interpret the
text in this or that way. Most preachers are pretty weak
here and prefer to be contemporary or inspiring rather
than scholarly. Scholarship, of itself, does not
necessarily convert or motivate. But if you are not
relying upon good scholarship, you will soon use your
private and often self-serving hermeneutic, and the Bible
means whatever you need it to mean. This is a problem
for both conservatives and liberals, unless they humbly
submit to their own limitations and partial perspectives.
If Scripture is always approached honestly, God is
always leading and in charge; we are always listeners and

learners. There's not much room for dogmatism or righteousness here. Just growth and maybe even that severe mercy called surrender.

So let me try to describe my masculine hermeneutic. There is nothing official about it. Others would say it differently, but these are the conclusions that I have come to in my years of work with men. We will look at these aspects of God that we characterize as "male," and how they are illustrated in Mary's visitation and Magnificat prayer. Most concisely and simply, I see authentic masculine spirituality as "the art of separation," which is one-half of the great mystery of love. It has to do with clarity and boundaries over too easy union. It has to do with journey from here to there, with self-possession, detachment and free decisions for and against. It has to do with outer over inner, action over more reflection, and a love of things, events and history itself over more concern for subjective states and feelings. Masculinity at its best is love for the whole, for the big picture and the entire narrative. It is self-sacrificing love over mere attachment or codependent small relationships. Finally, it is being quite comfortable with power, precisely because one has walked through powerlessness—and emerged unashamed. I cannot argue or prove these points here; it is beyond the scope of this essay. To settle your doubting spirit, I would just ask you to observe the great scriptures, myths and universal odysseys of history.

For our purposes here, let's see how Luke and Mary (We don't have to answer the question, "Whose words are they?" We leave that to the historical-critical folks!) represented these masculine biases in the Lucan account following the annunciation scene. We can rightly assume, however, that Luke's words are based upon some historical remembrance of the "real" Mary of Nazareth. If there is no historical ground, we get into fairy tales and the psyche becomes an unidentifiable flying object! I am convinced that the simple Mary of history would probably challenge and invite us much more than the "lovely lady dressed in blue" ever has. We are not into goddess religion with Mary. She is a woman of this earth, and that is more than enough. She is a woman who has integrated the best of feminine and masculine spirituality and, therefore, can speak for both.

First of all, the text begins with a going out (v. 39) and ends with a returning "back home" (v. 56). Upon receiving the sacred word, Mary does not contemplate, she *acts* immediately: "went as quickly as she could to a town in the hill country" (v. 39). There is no mention of planning, companionship, means of travel or encountered difficulties. Like Abraham and winged Mercury, she moved *with* the action, *toward* her cousin's need. The events themselves will be her guide and teacher. She does not need to figure it out and plan accordingly. The plan will be given by God through life's encounters. Reality is her teacher. That is why she could hear angels. And that is why she could hear Elizabeth.

Decisive action beyond our fears gives us a sense of our own power and the power of God within us. Mary offers no refusal or false humility to Elizabeth's "loud cry": "Of all women you are the most blessed....Yes, blessed is she who believes that the promise made her by the Lord would be fulfilled" (v. 42, 45). This is a woman who is profoundly self-possessed. She can hold her power comfortably because she knows it is from Beyond. She does not need to protect or deny it. It is hers to hold and offer, and as we will see in the next verses, to proudly proclaim. No codependent person here. This woman knows her boundaries, her Center and her gift. Her dignity is not earned or attained. It is. Mary is the lover and ultimate proclaimer of "Is-ness." With complete personal ownership, she begins, "My soul!" (v. 46) Yet the would-be inflation of religious experience is comfortably balanced with a clear knowledge of her personal is-ness: "his lowly handmaid" (v. 47), "the Almighty has done great things for me" (v. 48), [God has] "exalted the lowly" (v. 52). She is in her own estimate a recipient of "promise" and "mercy" (v. 54, 55). The entire prayer presents her as an amazing balance of surrender and responsibility, grace and ownership, holding in one utter powerlessness and total power. She stands as the archetype of liberated woman and liberating humanity. We all strive and hope for the same integration.

Within the ten verses of the Magnificat itself we see four liberations proclaimed: religious, social, political and economic. Her personal liberation underlies them all, which is most important to remember. She has allowed the truth within and so she can see the truth without. (1) Religiously, "his mercy reaches from age to age for those who live in awe of him" (v. 50). God's faithful love is not for any culticly correct group. It is universally available. Religiously inflated people don't want this liberation, as we see in all forms of pharisaism. (2) Socially, "he has routed those proud of heart" (v. 51). God is no respecter of persons, class or social pretense.

Yet all societies create their own symbols of dominance and superiority in terms of money, clothes, taste, accent and the self images that go with them. Mary says, forget it! (3) Politically, "he pulls down the mighty from their thrones and lifts up the lowly" (v. 52). No wonder the public proclamation of this prayer was actually banned for a short time in communist-fearing Argentina! Now that Marxism as a viable option is past, I must be free to say that Mary's words are obviously much closer to Karl Marx than to the trickle-down economists of the last fateful decade. (4) Economically, "he has filled the hungry with good things, and the rich he has sent away empty" (v. 53). Obviously, the preferential option for the poor was not discovered this century in Latin America. God clearly has a bias and a praxis. He *acts* on the side of the little guy. God *has* been in every war and revolution, fighting for and with the victims on *both* sides. That kind of God pleases no one in power. In the sense we use it here, Yahweh is uniquely a male God, who chooses, clarifies, decides, acts and holds power and powerlessness in balance. This is not a nurturing fertility goddess that Mary proclaims here. It is a reigning king God, who is nevertheless three times described as "Mercy" (v. 49, 45, 55) and "Savior" (v. 46) for us and all of our descendants. Mary is ready for the big picture, a part of all history. She is not interested in a tribal god offering her private good feelings of holiness.

In these passages we see a woman who is quite at home with the so called "male side" of God. She has seen the good side of power in "God's greatness" (v. 46) and is not naive about the dark side of power in her calls for liberation and justice. She is not afraid of it because she has it and knows its boundaries. In the end I think this is the characteristic of the full masculine. It is comfortable with power and knows how to use it for the common good. Many who are too anxious to throw out the male side of God are still afraid of or wounded by false power. But power (*dynamis*) is also a word for the Spirit, and it is the Holy Spirit that has "come upon" Mary (1:35). Liberals tend to mistrust and fear power; conservatives tend to avoid and hate powerlessness. Mary holds them both—together.

And like all great mythologies, the hero must finally return to the community with his newfound gift. Unless the man is reintegrated into the ordinary world, the world of family, love and loyalties, he is not a hero at all. In the woman Mary the pattern is a bit reversed. She goes out to help her cousin in her time of confinement and "returns back home" (v. 56) to bear her gift to the world. Perhaps the woman's way of bearing the masculine is to deal with the specific. Men look first for the great Love, leading them back to the specific.

You say, I don't see that happening! That is why we need a masculine spirituality. For both men and women.

22

Doing and Being

The strength of masculine energy is its power to attack.
We feel that power in the story of Iron John. The wild
man in each of us is a force for action, thrusting out into
the world and making things happen. The masculine
style puts doing over being. It prefers action in the world
to sitting back and thinking about it.

Although Catholic theology has for centuries been a
man's preserve, the actual way that theologians went
about their task was archetypally feminine. Since the
days of Thomas Aquinas and other scholastics in the
Middle Ages, theology has been done by sitting and
reading, thinking and reasoning, seeing the logical
connections between ideas and drawing conclusions
from them. It was a very sedentary activity that took
place not in the world of action but in a secluded
academic womb, be it a monastery, a university or a
seminary. This style of theology produced volumes of
books that could fill entire libraries, but very little of it
touched the daily lives of people or had much effect on
the world in which they lived.

Studying theology in that way did have a value in the

past, for it brought together Scripture, doctrine and philosophy in such a way as to provide the Church with an overall synthesis of revealed and human knowledge. That synthesis was part of the great Catholic worldview that informed the Christian tradition from the Middle Ages onward. As long as the world did not change, or change very rapidly, theologians could afford to take the ivory tower approach: They could sit back, observe and read, think and write, and what they said reflected the Christian understanding of the world as they knew it.

Today, however, that style of theology is becoming less and less relevant. The world is changing faster than armchair theologians can keep up with it, and it is changing in many directions simultaneously. Science, technology, life-styles, business, medicine, politics, economics, education and transportation (to name but a few areas) are continuously creating new opportunities and new problems with which Christians have to deal. Unemployment, homelessness, overconsumption, militarism, pollution, debt, depletion of resources, drugs and abortion present crises that theology addresses too late and with too little impact. Theology is not perceived as relevant to the way most people live.

One indication of this is the condition of the Church in Europe. We tend to think of Spain and Portugal, France and Italy as Catholic, but as a matter of fact the Church is almost dead in those countries. A recent statistic from Italy, to give but one example, is that only three percent of the people under age thirty-five seriously identify with the Catholic Church. Almost all of them are baptized and almost all of them want to have their children baptized, but almost none of them takes the teachings of their religion seriously. Except for being a cultural adornment, religion has become irrelevant.

Karl Rahner, the great German theologian of our century, said that by the next century the only people who will remain in the Church will be mystics. I take that to mean that unless people develop spiritually, religion is not going to make sense to them. And unless women and men perceive the Church as a place where spiritual development can happen, they will have little use for the Church.

Although we like to think that the Catholic Church fostered spiritual development in the past, this is not entirely true. The Church promoted spirituality only for that small percentage of Catholics who were priests or members of religious orders. The spirituality of the laity (if we might dignify it with such a title) was quite simply: Pray, pay and obey. Furthermore, clerical and religious spirituality was, as we have already seen, a feminine spirituality: Only the development of feminine virtues was considered important. Spiritual life in the past was therefore really spiritual half-life.

I can see this so clearly when I give retreats to priests, especially to older priests who underwent the traditional religious formation in their seminary years. Many of them are not able to trust themselves. They were told not to sin, or else God would not love them. In those days, though, any personal fault or shortcoming could be regarded as a sin, so the message they got was that it was a sin to make a mistake. It was better to do nothing than to make a mistake.

That type of emasculated spirituality effectively cut

out all risk taking from their lives. Although they prayed to God the Father in the Mass, they were often more devoted to Mary and the rosary. As a result, they never came in contact with the Father's masculine energy the way Jesus did. They never knew they had a wild man inside them or, if they did, they thought it was the devil tempting them to do something bad. They were effectively castrated, not only in their relationship to women but also in their ability to act decisively in the world.

Lest you think that I am putting priests down, I am quite aware that there have been magnificent exceptions to the rule. All the same, the exceptions are one thing and the rule is another. By and large, most priests have been company men, not wild men.

I am also quite aware that laypeople, men and women, also often fall into this pattern. This is even true of those who are trying to be spiritual, if the only spirituality they know is feminine spirituality. These are the people who are so concerned about their own spiritual house that they have no time to reach out to others. These are the ones who want to get it all together before they start giving it away. These are the type who criticize from the sidelines but never get into the action. They have all kinds of questions to ask, but they have nothing to contribute. They never make anything happen. They have no masculine energy.

Something very different is beginning to happen in the Third World. Taking their cue from Vatican II's *Constitution on the Church in the Modern World*, Latin American pastors and theologians decided to "read the signs of the times" and risk trying something new. They formed small base communities instead of the traditional large parishes. They relied on lay leadership instead of clerical control. Most interestingly, they threw out the traditional theology textbooks and brought the Scriptures to the people, asking them what the word of God meant to them.

Out of that decision to let God's word speak for itself—to let it name the goodness and the evil in the world and to suggest how to respond to it—what we know today as liberation theology was born. It is a theology that arises out of the experience of people and that shapes people's response to the situation in which they find themselves. It is a way of doing theology built on what they call *praxis*—practical activity informed by the message of the gospel. It is a much more grass roots way of theologizing which attacks problems at their roots and tries to find God in history, in events and in concrete action. It is a more masculine approach to theology than what the Church has had in the past.

Little wonder, then, that traditional theologians and conservative clergy reacted strongly to liberation theology when it first appeared. Many of the hierarchy apparently still do not understand it. Operating out of the feminine model of theology and spirituality, they view this truly different method as heretical. Comfortable with a passive theology and spirituality, they are upset with an aggressive, practical approach. Satisfied with a specialist's theology, they are bothered by a people's theology. Complacent with a company spirituality, they are unnerved when theology threatens to upset the apple cart.

Liberation theology, however, does not reach any

conclusions different from the fundamental doctrines of the Church or the basic teachings of the Scriptures. What it actually does is take those doctrines seriously and put those teachings into practice. It thereby transforms theology from just being something to read to being something to do—in the world. In other words, it taps into masculine energy and releases the explosive power of gospel.

The results are liberating. You have *everything* to be afraid of if you do *not* want to change your life.

Confrontation and Contemplation

Retreats are a good thing. It's good to get away from it all, to find some quiet time, to encounter the Lord. We need that time away from the demands and distractions of our daily routine so we can get into that space where we can just be, just reflect, just contemplate. If we never make a retreat, we may never find our center, or if we do, we may never spend much time there. Retreats are good for letting go of the shallow self—and moving into the deeper self.

For some people, however, making retreats has become a way of life. When the world gets to be too much for them, they make a retreat. When their friends are going, they go on a retreat. When a new spiritual director comes to town, they are anxious to hear what she or he has to offer. When they have nothing else to do, they make another retreat. They feel good about it for a while, and then their life is empty again.

Having seen folks like this come and go time after time, some retreat houses have made a rule that the only people they will admit are those who are engaged in some form of active service to others. They have come to the conclusion that those who never stretch between retreats never grow during retreats. In the name of searching for God, such would-be retreatants were actually running away from God. They were into religion, churchy things and pious practices, but they really weren't into God. The retreat houses didn't want to support that addiction to navel gazing and avoiding the deeper issues.

I think a better rule would be that for every retreat in your life, there should also be at least one "confront." There should be something you've come up against, something you've wrestled with, something you've tried to do in the world. If you've confronted some hardness in society, some evil in the world, some intransigence in the Church, then you have a reason to retreat and gather your inner strength. Then you have something to bring to the Lord in prayer and contemplation.

There needs to be a balance between the masculine and the feminine in the spiritual life. Making a retreat moves you into the feminine side, but spiritual growth cannot be just one-sided—for women *or* men. Unless there is a balance between retreats and confronts in your life, you deny the existence of the masculine side of the spiritual life. Unless there is some engagement in the world, some involvement in creating the kingdom of God, you deny the importance of masculine energy.

I would go even further. I would say that if you only think about Jesus and never act like Jesus, you are denying the mystery of the Incarnation. You are paying lip service to the Incarnation in your prayers, but you are denying it in your life. You are thinking about it in your head, but denying it in your life-style. We are converted by new circumstances much more than by new ideas.

The Incarnation was not a contemplative move on God's part but a confrontive move. It was a creative, masculine, seedplanting decision of God to get into the world and do something about it. It was the insertion—phallic, even—of God into humanity in the person of the man Jesus. That insertion came through the receptivity of a woman, to be sure; the Incarnation was accomplished *through* Mary *in* Jesus.

A mystery is not something to think about, it is something to live. We Catholics talk about participating in the mystery of the Incarnation, and even our catechism taught us that unless we participate in the mystery of Christ we cannot be saved. That is why I can say with confidence that unless you "walk your talk," unless you get into an incarnational life pattern, you are denying the Incarnation. You are saying it is not for you. You are denying that you really believe in it. To know and not to act is not to know.

The whole life pattern of Jesus—not just his birth—displays the meaning of Incarnation. In the Gospels we see God as a man in the person of Jesus inserting himself into people's lives, telling them what they need to hear—whether they want to listen or not. We see Jesus confronting the physical evil of sickness, the moral evil of sin, the spiritual evil of self-righteousness. And so he balances confrontation with retreat, going off into the hills to pray, finding the place where he and the Father are one. But he doesn't just contemplate. He doesn't just sit in his room and then come out and preach a sermon.

People are sick of sermons that come out of the study

and into the pulpit. Jesus' word, the Father's word, comes out of confrontation with the evil in the world. Jesus' life, the life of God incarnate, is a balance between confront and retreat, between action and contemplation. Which is why, when Jesus speaks, he speaks with authority, and people know he has something to say.

When I established the Center for Action and Contemplation in New Mexico, well-meaning folks asked if I had not put the words in the wrong order. Shouldn't "contemplation" come first, they asked. No, it was deliberate, I told them. We have nothing to contemplate beyond our self-centered position—until we have acted and moved beyond ourselves.

In my own life I have given hundreds of retreats and thousands of sermons. I know that when I talk, people sometimes get new ideas and they sometimes even get inspired. But they don't often get converted, they aren't really changed. It takes more than words to do that. What converts people are circumstances, real life situations. What changes people are confrontations, looking at something they don't want to deal with straight in the face, or looking at life from a new vantage point.

That's the way it was in my own life. When I joined the Franciscans as a boy, I had to face a seminary life which in those days had all the comforts of boot camp, and it changed me. When I got the one assignment I asked not to be given—working with teenagers—I faced up to it, and it changed my life. When that retreat work made me face the fact that more than sermons and prayer meetings were needed, it led me into founding the New Jerusalem community. That whole new living experience demanded one conversion after another, not only for me but for everyone else in the community. Finally, when I got called to give talks in the Third World, I had to confront the reality of that situation, and it forced me into further conversion. Reality has a way of making you have to deal with it. Reality is the greatest ally of God. What *is* converts us. That is full incarnation.

For much of our Catholic lives we were warned to avoid the near occasions of sin. I think it's time we began inserting ourselves in near occasions of grace. We need to put ourselves in situations where we are forced to do a complete about-face. That's what conversion basically means: turning around. At the very least, we need to move out of our white, middle-class ghetto and confront the dark underworld of poverty on which it floats. We need to see, not how the other *half* lives, but how the other ninety percent of the people in the world are forced to live.

Every viewpoint is a view from a point. And your view depends on the point where you stand. If you stand at the top of the heap, you can't see, feel or experience life the way it is at the bottom. The people at the top can afford to be conservative. They've made it, so they really have no felt need for change or reform. They don't feel the pinch. They have the power, so they use it to preserve and defend. They have the leisure, so they can dabble in religion and go on retreats.

The people at the bottom don't have the luxury of being conservative. They have to push for change. They have to make new things happen. They have to confront the reality that they've been handed—the dead-end jobs, the run-down housing, the crime in the streets, the drugs in the schools—and face it head-on. If they are not to be crushed by it, they have to fight it. They have to struggle for liberation. They have to get in touch with masculine energy, and be creative.

If we believe that the view from the top is the whole of reality, we are not living in the real world. If we believe that life is good to the majority of people, we are naively optimistic. If we believe that everyone is free like us, we are trapped. If we believe that we have everything we need, we have lost our soul.

If we want to be fully men, we have to feel the pain of the world. We have to grieve over the darkness inside us and the dark world around us.

We do not convert ourselves. We are converted—by the push and tug of the real—and usually in spite of ourselves.

24

Man the Seed Bearer

"The seed of a pear tree grows into a pear tree,
the seed of a nut tree grows to be a nut tree,
the seed of God grows to be God."
        —Meister Eckhart[24]

Every man needs to be a source of creation. In every masculine soul there is a desire to be a source of new life. Men want in their hearts to express themselves outwardly and to be respected for that. Unless they can be generative and creative, men don't feel good about themselves. And it is precisely for their masculine generativity that men are honored and respected by other men and women.

Recently, a young woman told me that she was breaking up with her boyfriend, and when I asked her why, she said it was because he never did anything on his own. He never took the initiative, either in their relationship or in the rest of his life. He was always a

---

[24]Eckhart, Meister. "Of the Nobleman," *Meister Eckhart: The Essential Sermons, Treatises, and Defense*, eds. Edmund Colledge and Bernard McGinn. N.Y.: Paulist Press/SPCK, 1981, p. 241.

follower, never a doer. She was the one who always had to suggest things to do and places to go. He was always attentive and caring, and he was always considerate and cooperative, but he never came up with a new idea and asked her to go along. Slowly she lost respect for him as a man, and in the end, she pitied him.

I know a number of women who pity their husbands. They cannot admire them because they never do anything to arouse their wives' admiration. The men go to work and come home dutifully every day. They take out the garbage and do whatever the wives ask them to do, but that's the extent of their energy. I have no idea how the men are in bed, but I suspect they don't surprise their wives there, either. Perhaps the men's initiative has been beaten down or driven out of them, but it's not there. So the wives love them, but they do not respect their husbands as men.

In our society biology has become destiny, so to speak. Our sex gives direction to our lives. For men, it means carrying and planting seeds. For women, it means receiving and protecting what is planted. This is not to say that men haven't any need to nurture what they have created, or that women haven't any ability to create. But it is to say that what is written in our genes is also written in our souls as men and women. And the deepest inscription in the masculine soul is to procreate.

Biologically speaking, masculine energy is not just phallic but also scrotal. It is important to recognize that most vulnerable, tender and protected part of a man, his testicles, as an essential part of his power. Otherwise, all of men's nonphallic attributes are projected onto women and expected to be carried by women. For too long, women have done the feeling and the nurturing for the family. We long to know what "male-feeling" feels like. Most of us go to women for nurturance because we cannot imagine receiving it from a man. Yet men have scrotal, or testicular, energy too: a quiet, hidden seed, a uniquely masculine capacity for containment and protection, patient ripening, rootedness and long-term endurance. Even the penis is soft and still much more than it is hard and intent.

The same part of the male anatomy is both most protected and most powerful. An exaggerated phallic energy, uninformed by scrotal energy, is usually a sign of an intrusive, domineering and exploitive male. It is macho overcompensation rather than true masculine self-confidence. The drivenness of the businessman, the sterility of the academic, the rigidity of the believer, the war games of the military, the stabbing finger of the opinionated, the punishing inner father—these are all indications of the phallic man, not the true wild man. The true wild man has life for others and *knows* that he has life for others!

Theologically speaking, masculine energy is the energy of God the creator. When we experience ourselves as givers of life, we know God the Father—not conceptually but experientially. Our giving spirit is the Father's creative spirit moving through us. That creative spirit is what we theologically name the Holy Spirit. God dwells within us and that divine indwelling is felt as the spiritual energy to create.

This desire to be a source of creation is our deepest identification with God the Father. It expresses itself in the desire for fatherhood, whether it be to have children in the usual physical sense or to have spiritual children in the sense of fostering growth and maturity in others. My desire to speak and to write in order to give birth to something new in the lives of others, for example, expresses my own deepest need to be a father, to be an author of new life.

A Jewish rabbi once made much the same point in speaking about prayer. When I pray, he said, I am God. That's a bold way to put it, but it's just another way of talking about what Jesus meant when he said, "I and the Father are one." It is our experienced identification with God the Father. When prayer moves beyond the stage of talking to God, it becomes unification with God. Our felt unity with God is our oneness with God in the Spirit. The Spirit moves us to prayer, and if we stick with it, the Spirit leads us beyond asking God for favors to the realization that the divine energy to do what we asked in prayer is within us.

Sometimes I wonder if this dynamic truth is not at the heart of the common male practice of playing catch with dad—and the source of a gnawing sense of deprivation if it never happened.

At our Baptism we were told that we are sons of God, but most of us do not really believe it. We think we have to merit the Father's love, even though we do not. We think we have to be good and earn Daddy's approval, even though it has already been given to us. Trying to be worthy in the eyes of God is the exact opposite of the good news of the Scriptures, which was first announced to us at our Baptism. Our holiness is inherent and recognized, not earned.

We do not have to become sons of God; we *are* sons

of God. From the moment of our Baptism, we are both human and divine. What was once interior to God, within the Trinity, is now exteriorized in us. The mystery of the Trinity is ours by grace, through the gift of Baptism. We are adopted sons of God, but we are sons really no less than Jesus was. We do not need to spend our efforts trying to earn what we already have by spiritual birth.

The seed is already the plant. Spirituality is a matter of allowing and becoming what we already are.

25

God as Paradox:
Powerful Powerlessness

A striking portrayal of the father-son relationship I have been describing hangs in a most unlikely place—although it's not that unlikely when you consider the

Christian interest in the Trinity. I came across it in the Cistercian monastery of Heilsbronner Muenster in Germany, where it hangs above the Marian altar. The painting impressed me so profoundly that I bought a copy of it for my study, and every time I looked at it I saw more and more in it. The insight of its painter, Sebastian Dayg, an almost unknown artist of the early sixteenth century, into the relationship between the Father and the Son still impresses me.

Picture if you will the stereotypical figure of God the Father. He's a stern old man with a flowing gray beard, and in his left hand he holds the orb which in medieval times symbolized kingly power. If you look more closely, though, you see that the orb of power is slipping from his hand. God the Father, the supreme authority figure, is supposedly in control of the whole world, and yet actually he has let go of that control. He is certain enough of his own power that he can let go of it. He is so certain of his own authority that he doesn't have to manipulate. He is self-possessed enough that he can allow for freedom.

At the same time that the Father allows us our freedom, he is also demanding. This is symbolized in the painting by a large sword that the Father holds in his right hand, wielding it over his head. This is the expectant and exacting side of God, summoning us to use well the freedom he has given us and challenging us to be all that we can be. In human fathers it's a kind of love that pushes and won't put up with excuses. It's a very masculine, tough love. That's a very modern concept, but this artist saw it in God almost five centuries ago.

The other side of God in the Trinity is the Son. In the painting this is symbolized by Jesus, stripped almost naked and still wearing the crown of thorns. If the Father is the strong and demanding side of God, the Son is the weak and suffering side, the part of God that identifies with our brokenness and even with our sinfulness. God asks a lot of us, but God also knows our feebleness and limitations. In the painting the Father is looking into the Son's eyes and the Son is looking into the Father's eyes in perfect reciprocity and mutual understanding.

As if to emphasize his human weakness, Jesus' right hand is in the bleeding wound in his side, but his left hand reaches up and grabs the sword that is poised above the head of these two figures. The Son holds back the sternness of the Father and prevents it from being too severe, so that the toughness and tenderness of God are in perfect balance. Symbolizing this balance, the sword itself is perfectly horizontal. If the Father is the powerful side of God, the Son is the vulnerable side. The two are in perfect tension, the Father in this painting representing the powerlessness of divine power and the Son representing the power of divine powerlessness. The creative energy that tension releases is symbolized by the dove of the Holy Spirit which, appropriately enough, hovers on the balanced sword. It is this same kind of creative energy that is released when strength and gentleness understand and respect each other, whether that balance is struck between a man and a woman or between the masculine and feminine sides within an individual.

But that's only half the picture. In this painting the Trinity are off to the left side, and across the space in the middle stands a woman. She is Mary who, in medieval art, symbolizes the whole Church because in relation to the creative masculinity of God, humanity is receptively feminine. Her eyes gaze not at any one of the Trinity but toward the space in the center, as if contemplating the whole mystery. A faint smile suggests she is admiring and respecting what she beholds, letting God be God. Yet her right hand is touching her breast, as if to indicate she knows that part of God was and still is within her.

The woman is dressed in a long gown and a flowing cape, and with her left hand she is holding up the cape to shield the figures standing behind her. Those figures are all men of power, prelates bedecked in vestments and tiaras and miters and kings with their crowns and symbols of authority. Unlike the woman, these men are not looking at the Trinity. They are gazing in every direction but God, which tells me that the artist knew that men of power get so caught up in their roles and privileges that they lose sight of God. So in one sense Mary is protecting them from the Father's sword, but in another she is telling them that they are not ready for the mystery of God's tough and tender love. Only one joins the Eternal Feminine in her gaze, the one with bowed head and folded hands.

The painting as a whole, then, depicts the father-son relationship as a creative tension between forcefulness and woundedness. Only the woman who has integrated the masculine within herself has the strength to stand before the Trinitarian power of God. And only the centered man who has integrated the feminine within himself joins her in recognition and acceptance of the divine paradox.

After reflecting on this wonderful painting for many years now, I honestly wonder how comfortable Christianity is with its Christ. If I am to believe much of our Church agenda, then this wounded half of God must be an embarrassment and a serious threat. The other powerful side of God has been used far too much to enforce our own cultural and private issues. Mary, it seems, is ready for the whole paradox. Humanity stands behind her left arm, waiting to see.

>>> **26** <<<

Spiritual Fathering: Male Mothering

When we men are deprived of authentic brotherhood, we seek substitutes in the company and praise of other men, in transitory experiences of camaraderie and in games where we can feel like team players.

Our woundedness as men can only be healed through an experience of union. It can be the experience of identification with our own fathers. It can be the experience of oneness with God, such as Jesus knew it. Or it can be an experience of unity within ourselves.

Normally—since father hunger is the norm in our culture—we do not come to such healing on our own. Since our wholeness is not given to us by our natural fathers, we have to receive it through spiritual fathering. We need a mentor, we need a "male mother" through whom we can receive that masculine energy which will awaken our own. We need a man to be in solidarity with us, so that we can learn what it means to be in solidarity with others.

Interestingly enough, the biological father is hardly ever the initiator of his own son. There is too much tension in the relationship. For one thing, they are both in love with the same woman. Older and unrelated males are almost always the initiators of the boy into manhood. The mother leads the son through boyhood, but other men must "kill the boy softly" so that the man can emerge. We have no rite or easy possibility of this in our culture. We *must* learn how. We men owe it to ourselves and future generations.

Eastern religions, even eastern orthodox Christianity, are much more aware of this need than we in the western Church have been. When the time comes for a boy in the East to take his spiritual development seriously, he is given a mentor, a master, a guru—not so much that he can learn facts or doctrines from him, but so that he can pick up the energy of his teacher by observation and by identification with him.

It is strange how we have forgotten that that's exactly the way Jesus formed his disciples. We can read all the words of Jesus in the Gospels in a matter of hours, but Jesus spent three long years discipling the men who followed him. What he gave them was not so much his words but his example and his energy. The New Testament word for that energy was "spirit."

Whether we are conscious of it or not, we do pick up on other people's energy. We might describe it as a personality to which we are attracted or from which we are repelled. We might say we like a person's character or are turned off by his or her temperament. Very often it is not so much that we react to what is said, but rather to the spirit of the person, the spirit in which it is said. Two people can hold the same opinion, but we feel invited to accept it when one of them presents it and we feel cold and unmoved when we hear it from the other.

It's not the idea that is different, but the energy behind it.

Women are generally much more attuned to such energy than we men are. Their woman's intuition, as it is called, perceives nonverbal cues and senses the spirit in a person much more readily than we do. We men live so much in our heads (which is just another way of saying that we spend much more time thinking with the left brain) that we are not aware that we respond to other people's energy. We believe we are being totally rational, yet all the while we are unconsciously reacting to the energy we receive from others.

The more we develop our feminine side, though, the better we become at tuning in to the energy around us. We learn to sense what is going on beneath the surface. We learn to read between the lines. We learn to respond to what people are trying to say when they speak to us. We learn to catch their meaning even if they are not saying it the way our logical minds like to hear it.

The danger in developing our feminine side, however, is that we can become overly sensitive to the energies around us, especially the negative energies from criticism and rejection. That negativity brings us down to a low point, and we have a hard time finding the deep masculine energy to respond to it positively. We fall easily into the shallow masculine and want to fight back, or we fall into the shallow feminine and want to cry and run away. When we cannot reach the deep masculine within us, we need spiritual fathering.

A priest to whom I was a sort of spiritual father once came to see me because he was in precisely this kind of crisis. Some people in his parish were constantly objecting to many of the things he did, pointing out when he did not follow the rubrics for the liturgy exactly, protesting when he talked about social concerns in his sermons, complaining that he did not put enough emphasis on Catholic doctrine, threatening to write to the bishop and so on. He was being bombarded by negative energy and at a certain point it began to get to him. He was losing the enthusiasm he had brought to that parish, he was beginning to feel anger and fear infecting his ministry, he was doubting his gifts as a priest and his abilities as a man. It takes a very strong man to withstand constant criticism.

First and foremost, this priest needed someone to just listen to him, to allow him to express his fears and frustrations, his anger and self-doubt. He also needed some reassurance from someone who had walked the journey ahead of him that what he was experiencing was normal and that it was possible to deal with it. He was needing to hear from someone like a grandfather, someone who had been there before and who could assure him that he was not crazy. He needed to "feel" from another man's experience what boundaries were worth protecting and what boundaries didn't really matter.

The eastern religious traditions, as I said above, make more provision for this need than our own does. After I had given a retreat in Nepal, I was given the opportunity to meet a Hindu guru, a spiritual teacher or wise man. As soon as I entered his small house, almost like a hermitage, on the outskirts of Katmandu, I was aware of being in the presence of something I could only call grandfather energy. When I talked with him, I had the distinct impression that he knew ahead of time everything I was bringing up. He had walked the journey ahead of me and he was far more advanced in the spiritual life than I was, so he simply recognized the confusions I brought to him and he confirmed many of the insights I had about spiritual growth.

While we talked, I noticed a picture of his own teacher, the guru who had been a spiritual father and grandfather to him. Whenever he mentioned his teacher, his eyes brightened with excitement. At one point he explained to me that the entire Hindu tradition of spirituality was built on a father-son relationship. As if to remind the pupil of the importance of this relationship, tradition requires that whenever he comes into the presence of his guru he should kneel and bow down, saying, "May I be so humble before you, my spiritual father, that even the dust can crush me." A very poetic greeting, to be sure, but it makes space for an immense trust relationship that allows power and energy, particularly masculine energy, to pass from one man to another.

On another occasion, I was talking with Jim Wallis, the pastor of the Sojourners community in Washington, D.C. Jim and I have a lot in common since we are about the same age, we are both founders of communities and we have experienced many of the same ups and downs in our ministries during the years. Jim made the observation that one of the hardest things about being in our position is that there are no father figures around for us. There are no men who have founded and pastored alternative Christian communities and who have already been through what we're going through. We find ourselves in the first generation of a Church that is very different from the way the Church has been for centuries. The usual rules of parish life don't apply to us in many cases, and we find ourselves having to invent an entirely new set of rules, learning by trial and error. Sometimes, he admitted, he'd like to be able to let it all hang out in front of someone who could just sit there and listen calmly, while he was panicking. I had to agree with him.

Even men in ordinary parish ministry—and I'm sure that this is equally true of men in the business world—need someone with authority who can let them know that it's OK, that what they're going through is normal, that they're doing a fine job. We all need to be assured from time to time that what we're doing is the right thing. We are not sure where we stand because no one is there to reassure us. Sometimes we just need to hear from someone who believes in us, but who believes in us enough to also challenge us. Suddenly, the assurance and self-confidence are there, almost by magic, and almost embarrassingly so. It is humbling and wonderful to be a spiritual son.

Indeed, I have no doubt that one of the main reasons I have done some interesting things in my life is that I have known a number of men who believed in me throughout my formation. I remember one older friar who told me as a young Franciscan: "Richard, I want you always to trust your intuitions. Promise me that you will always trust them, even if they are wrong once in a while. The direction is right and I will personally fight for you in the background if it ever comes to that." Need I say more? He was God for me—he was my spiritual father. And one spiritual father can make up for thousands of negative demons.

Ultimately, though, if we are listening to the Spirit, we are led into uncharted territory, and we find ourselves in a space where there is no one else around who can give us the security we are looking for. At times like that, we have to do as Jesus did and seek the guidance and assurance of the Father. When we have no spiritual father to help us, we need to turn to God for help. That is the meaning of the forty days in the desert.

Even St. Francis in the first years after his youthful conversion was not strong enough to overcome the pain of his father's rejection. He needed the assurance of another that he was God's and he was good.

> When his [Francis'] father saw him in this
> pitiful plight, he was filled with sorrow, for
> he had loved him very dearly; he was both
> grieved and ashamed to see his son half-dead
> from penance and hardships, and whenever
> they met, he cursed Francis. When the
> servant of God heard his father's curses, he
> took as his father a poor and despised outcast
> and said to him: "Come with me and I will
> give you the alms I receive; and when I hear
> my father cursing me, I shall turn to you
> saying 'Bless me, Father'; and then you
> will sign me with the cross and bless me in his
> place." And when this happened, the beggar
> did indeed bless him; and Francis turned to
> his father, saying, "Do you not realize
> that God can give me a father whose blessing

will counter your curses?"[25]

A few months earlier he had stripped naked in the city square, returned the clothes to his greedy father and said, "From now on I will say 'Our Father who art in heaven,' and not Father Pietro Bernardone." But the pain of that rejection and denial was never gone from his life. It determined the ferocity of his attitude toward money, his need and capacity for loving brothers and his bottomless desire for union with a heavenly Father. But the absence was still there, and the wound became a gift: the very feminine, poetic, intuitive spirituality of St. Francis. I suspect there is not such a gift without a wound. Yet the wound must be recognized, wept over and blessed.

We cannot wait until we are in a crisis to turn to God, however. We need to find that space where we and the Father are one and get used to going there regularly so that he can give us divine energy not only to meet emergencies but also to create opportunities. If we are in solidarity with the Father and allow ourselves to be spiritually fathered from day to day, God gives us the courage to take risks, the strength to carry through and the confidence to father others on their own journeys.

[25]"Legend of the Three Companions," #23, *St. Francis of Assisi Writings and Early Biographies: English Omnibus of the Sources for the Life of St. Francis*, ed. Marion A. Habig and trans. Brown, R., B. Fahy, P. Hermann, P. Oligny, N. de Robeck, L. Sherley-Price. Chicago, Ill.: Franciscan Herald Press, 1973.

>>> **27** <<<

The Young Boy and the Old Man

Depth psychology, which in some respects is a modern secular version of traditional spirituality and deals with many of the same issues, tells us that our lives are often guided by subconscious images called archetypes. Carl Jung claims that some of these archetypes are so basic to our lives as human beings they are found in people all over the world. These fundamental patterns show up in dreams and behavior in every culture, and they appear in symbols and stories that go as far back in time as we want to go. Other psychologists note that there are also archetypes more related to specific cultures and particular situations. Sometimes these are stereotypes of what it means to be a man or woman—what we have called the common masculine and the common feminine in our society. Sometimes these are self-images we develop as children—like when we see ourselves as helpless because our parents were always telling us that we couldn't do anything right.

Two of the more fundamental archetypes underlying male consciousness are the young boy and the old man, the inner child and the inner grandfather. They are both found in each of us to varying degrees, and in our life cycle we hope to journey from one to the other. Some men, unfortunately, overidentify with one archetype and, hence, become compulsive and unbalanced personalities. Interestingly, though, as we head toward the end of the journey, the two normally are integrated, and in our old age we are able to complete the circle and regain much of the freshness and freedom of youth, as well as the serenity and wisdom of old age.[26]

Some of us grew up too soon; some of us never grew up. One is called the old man, the other is called the eternal boy. We need them both. The old man *will not* change without contact with his eternal boy; the eternal boy *cannot* change without the love and challenge of his old man. Traditional religion and schooling tended to create and reward old men as does the success-oriented business world. Apart from art and music, there is very little to create and reward the eternal boy in us. Even sports in its competitive mode creates old men. True religion should be the harmonious integration of both. One without the other is destructive. Let's make the complementary gifts very clear:

The Eternal Boy	The Old Man
Action that does not know	Knowledge that does not act
Fanatic	Cynic
Change	Continuity
Hopes, expects, ready to be surprised	Holds, knows, loves, in control
Power of powerlessness (Jesus)	Powerlessness of power (The Father)
The energy of the wound	The energy to wound
Transcedent, hopeful, visionary	Immanent, grounded, remembering
Authenticity	Reality

[26]For a more complete description of the archetypes of the young boy and the old man, read John A. Sanford and George Lough, *What Men Are Like* (Paulist Press, 1988), pp. 95-97.

Fun and fantasy	Work and responsibility
Inspires the blossoming of things	Knows how to gather the harvest
All space, no time (too much heaven)	All time, no space (too much earth)

The critical age is often in the forties, when the two archetypes usually confront one another. Usually one is rejected forever. Because of the sophistication and success needs of our culture, most men reject the eternal boy and substitute it with cheap recreation and travel. Those who choose the eternal boy end up artists, revolutionaries, misfits or religious rebels, usually considered naive or useless. We are heavily weighted to one side without knowing it.

All through our lives, however, both archetypes are already present. At certain stages and in certain circumstances we tend to favor one or the other, sometimes behaving childishly and enjoying it, at other times being more serious than our years require of us. As I look back on my own life, I'd have to say that I identified strongly with the old man even when I was fairly young. I did not participate in sports because I felt there were things of greater consequence which I should be attending to. When I was in the seminary, my classmates picked up on this fatherly side of me and I often found myself being asked for counsel and advice.

People who know me even today notice that I don't have any jokes to chip in when everybody's sharing jokes and that I don't tell funny stories the way that other preachers and retreat masters do. Somehow I never learned to tell jokes and I'm sometimes limited by that inability. I love other people who are funny and I admire them because I can't be like that. That's what the old man does: He admires in the little boy what he does not have. And the boy in turn admires the old man for being what he himself is not. I don't mean to imply that I can't relax and have fun. I enjoy letting my child out as much as any man does, but in me the little boy has to ask the grandfather's permission, so to speak, and be assured that it's OK to play once in a while.

Even though because of personality or situation we might find ourselves favoring the boy or the old man in us, both archetypes are in each one of us. Again, it is not a matter of either/or but a matter of both/and. Both the child and the grandfather have gifts to give us, and we need to appreciate both in order to enjoy our full giftedness as men. So even though I will talk about these two in terms of contrasts, we need to remember that the two are just different aspects of a balanced masculinity.

The young boy is hopeful and optimistic; the old man is knowledgeable and certain. To the boy, life is waiting out there to be lived; to the old man, life is the experience of having lived. Many of us cross that boundary in middle age, when we realize that most of our life has already happened, and we find ourselves reminiscing more about the past than expecting great things in the future. If the little boy has been unduly denied, he will make a strong, almost irresistible appeal in mid-life. It is a crisis of major proportions for many men in their forties.

So the boy is full of wonder and awe, but the old man is full of recognition. I can remember one time when I was traveling in a van with a group of young people from New Jerusalem. They were all from Cincinnati, and they had never been west of Indiana, but here we were together, heading for the far west. As we got to where we ought to be able to catch our first glimpse of the Rockies, they all crowded into the front of the van, waiting for the mountains to appear. Their eyes were like little children's, wondering what would happen next. I remember feeling a kind of envy for those kids; I had seen the mountains so many times that I had lost the ability to be surprised by them. But I also felt something that the young people could not feel. When the mountains at last came into view, I recognized them as old friends.

Another contrast is between credulity and credibility. The little boy is credulous because he has not yet learned enough to be able to tell what's true from what isn't. In that sense, he is naive, but his is the refreshing naïveté of the child who can listen and accept with openness. He believes what he hears because he trusts the person who is speaking to him. He follows what he is told to do because he is willing to try new things and learn from experience that he himself has not yet had.

The grandfather, on the other hand, is the bestower of knowledge and the giver of advice which comes out of his own experience. He is credible because he knows firsthand what he is talking about. He is believable because he lives according to what he says. He is therefore an authority because he authors new possibilities in the lives of those who listen to him, and his authorship comes not from what he has heard but from what he has lived.

The next difference has to do with what psychologists call the shadow, or the unseen and unacceptable side of one's personality.

Since the boy is young and does not know himself, he

has a large shadow. He does things he does not understand and he reacts to situations in ways which he is not in control of. The child's shadow often gets projected on to other children and adults since he does not yet understand human behavior and he has not yet learned to look at things from other people's viewpoints. He is both critical and afraid of those around him, and he reacts unthinkingly to situations rather than responding to them out of knowledge.

The old man, by contrast, has been around a long time and he has seen all there is to see. He understands the ways that people act and he is not thrown off by them. More importantly, he knows himself, and there is little anyone can criticize him for which he is not already aware of. He has drawn his own shadow into the light of consciousness, and so he has the psychological space to absorb the shadowy manipulations of others. And by not projecting anything on to other people, he can give them the room they need to just be themselves.

Maybe I can best illustrate this with an incident that happened not too long ago. I was talking with a man in New Jerusalem who had joined the community when he was still in high school and who still had a hard time with relationships. Now, that puzzled me, since in our own relationship we always seemed to get along well together. For some reason or another, he started telling me about how his friends, and especially his girlfriend, were unhappy with him. They felt he was being manipulative and he himself felt there were aspects of his personality that grated on other people's nerves.

After listening to him for a while, I confessed to him that I had never felt him being manipulative and I had never seen him doing the kinds of things he was accusing himself of. He looked at me wistfully and said, "Around you, my shadow never shows itself. Come to think of it, you're the only person I know who makes it unnecessary for me to behave the way I usually do with others. Somehow, you have the ability to free me from my moods and fears—that whole negative side of me—and let me be the person I would really like to be." The old man has the magical power to absorb the shadow of the boy. The grandfather makes it possible for a person to leave his darkness aside and walk in the light that he knows is there but can't easily find.

Still another difference between the boy and the old man involves the way men give and receive love. A father's love, as we saw earlier, is pushing and challenging, tossing the eaglets out of the nest and telling them they can fly. The son, of course, recognizes the father's concern for him, but he is not always sure where dad is coming from. So the young boy represents love that is *wounded,* and the old man represents love that is *willing to wound.*

When I went to Japan, I was told that a young man never knows what's going to happen to him when coming to join a Zen Buddhist community. Sometimes an aspiring monk would knock on the monastery door. And sometimes he'd even have to wait two or three days before they would let him in, to check out how badly he really wanted to be converted and grow in the spiritual life. Now, there's manly energy from day one! And the life of the novice in the monastery is just as tough. It's very disciplined and very challenging.

The young boy, for his part, is willing to let himself

be wounded because he trusts the old man's love for him. Countless boys let countless coaches force them to stretch to the limits of their endurance because they want what the man can call forth in them. In my own life, that place of manly testing was the seminary. I arrived in Cincinnati from Kansas when I was only fourteen and I had to find my way from the train station, Union Terminal, to the Franciscan friary, about fifteen miles away, by bus. The bus delivered me to the closest stop, where there was no one there to meet me. So I trudged with my two suitcases up the mile-long road to the friary feeling all alone and scared to death.

I can identify with what I hear about Zen monasteries because seminaries in the years before Vatican II were not much different. They got us up in the cold (and sometimes dark) early morning for prayer and meditation. The rules were strict, and our lives were pretty regimented to a degree that I sometimes resented and in ways, looking back, that were not really necessary. But they weren't all that bad, either. One thing the old-fashioned seminary did for many of us was it made us take a good hard look at ourselves and ask what we were really there for. We weren't there for our own comfort, that's for sure! I suppose that other young men have had similar experiences in other places, such as the army or the football team.

Often they merely brutalize and desensitize the young man, but the father-as-wounder also has a very special gift for the receptive son. It is the polar opposite of the nurturing mother, but gives a necessary container and form and capacity for self-criticism that can be found nowhere else.

The eternal boy is often angry at the old man for giving him the very gifts that could make him great. As a man said to me at the jail just today, "It takes us such a long time to grow up and become wise, Father, and by then we have already made all of our life's decisions and all of our mistakes."

The eternal boy and the old man will always need one another. Perhaps this is why the very last verse of the Old Testament promises and offers the eternally returning Elijah: "[t]o turn the hearts of the father to their children and the hearts of the children to their fathers" (Malachi 3:24).

28

Soul Images for Men

"Four Mighty Ones are in every man. A
perfect unity cannot exist but from the
universal brotherhood of Eden."
            —William Blake, *The Four Zoas*

Since we have introduced the idea of archetypes that
form and fascinate the souls of men, I would like to offer
you some classic images from literature and mythology
and what I believe is the collective male unconscious.
There are four classic images that continue to appear in
every age. Robert Moore, who is doing the definitive
studies in this area, calls them: the king, the warrior, the
magician and the lover.[27]

I have found these so helpful in recent retreat work
and jail ministry that I would like to share some of what
we are learning in a condensed form. Enough I hope, so
you can listen to your own unconscious with new trust
and awareness.

First, I would like to say something about

---

[27]Moore, Robert and D. Gillette. *King Warrior Magician Lover*. San Francisco:
HarperSanFrancisco, 1990.

archetypes. The Swiss psychologist, Carl Jung, believed that true transformation of persons happened largely, if not exclusively, through contact with images. Some of these images have an almost luminous character for us. Like meeting a god, they can both frighten and fascinate us. So much so, in fact, that they can guide and determine what we pay attention to, and often blind us to their dark sides. A young man caught up in a warrior archetype, for example, sees everything through the eyes of winning, muscles, size, power and domination. It has little to do with logic or training, and warnings against violence will do little good: He is possessed by a god (or a demon, depending on how you see it).

Archetypal fascinations would seem like more psycho-babble to me if I had not seen the power of stories, icons, biographies, pictures, movies, celebrities and heroes in peoples' lives. We can preach, talk and write all we want, but it is self-evident to me that people change people. Until this very day that I write, the AIDS epidemic was largely distant and abstract for most Americans. Magic Johnson, the basketball player, announced yesterday that he was infected, and the entire country is ablaze with fear, recognition and what some are calling the final nail in the coffin of the sexual revolution. That is the almost imperial power of an archetype. I know very few, if any, people who have been converted by theology itself. Lives of the saints, meeting a saint, the stories of the Gospels and heroism can turn us around in one minute—and forever.

Archetypes are filled with generative power. They lead us into "sacred space" where we "see" for the first time. We understand, we know what we must do, and somehow in the fascination we even find the energy to do it. When you are in the grip of an archetype, you have vision and a deep sense of meaning for your life, even if it is just to be the best break-dancer in Brooklyn! We speak of being "possessed" by an archetype with probably the same meaning that the ancients spoke of being possessed by a devil. If you don't recognize it and somehow respect or exorcise it, you will likely overidentify with it. It gets you! The archetype must be honored for what it is, an image outside of the self that calls us to growth, change and awareness. In its negative form it can equally call us to evil and destruction. That is why you must know your own center, which is the purifying and ego-stripping function of all healthy religion.

The central masculine archetypes seem to always be about *power*: how is power good, how is power contained, how is power shared, how is power used for others, what is spiritual power and what is selfish power. What characterizes the *puer*, or the uninitiated boy, is that he is usually naive about power. He mistrusts it, and if he has had no proper male modeling, he even hates it and uses every chance he can to show his disdain for power and authority. The *puer eternus*, of course, never grows out of this stage, and that is much of the human race. The irony is that he himself desires and seeks power, but just in different and disguised forms. The male *must* learn the good name for power. He must honor it, or it will almost always destroy him. Witness most of the Greek and Shakespearian tragedies.

Because we have not done our inner work, listened to our stories and initiated the younger men, power is largely out of control and universally mistrusted in western society. Our sisters are often convinced that patriarchy ("the rule of the fathers") is identical with maleness, and maleness is always about domination, war, greed and control. We have to show them and ourselves that maleness *is* about power, but power for good, power for others, power for life and creativity. Power cannot be inherently evil. One word for the Holy Spirit in the New Testament is *dynamis* or power. All the legends and myths of history cannot be wrong. Warriors are not going to stop fascinating young boys because feminist mothers don't like it or pacifists rail against it. Like most of the great world religions, we just have to discover the meaning of the spiritual warrior.

With all that said, let us look at our four numinous male images. I say numinous intentionally because there is something about these figures, when we rightly meet them, that opens us up to the Holy, the transcendent, or at least our very deepest self.

The King

This image includes the Father images and carries all the connotations of authority, order, law, direction and grounding. The calm king sitting on his throne is the archetype of centeredness and security within himself. He is, therefore, a symbol of fertility and creativity for all those within his realm. To be in the king's good graces is to be OK at the core. The king center in a man is secure enough to recognize, affirm and bless goodness when he sees it in others. He is not threatened by the growth or maturity of others, because he knows and loves who he himself is. You cannot threaten the king because he does not need you, or even need your admiration. He is the principle of healthy autonomy and very clear boundaries. The greater the king, the bigger the realm he can hold together. Some are kings for their own limited racial group, some hold together a "rainbow coalition," others preside over the whole domain and hold it together in unity. Thus Christians rightly speak of Jesus as "King of kings."

The Shadow King

Each image has a clear dark side in mythology. Jesus, for example, often builds parables around evil kings. This is the image of impotence and paranoia. He is threatened by others' power and creativity, with a childish sense of his own importance. It is interesting that both Herod and Pilate are usually pictured this way in movies, clearly drawing upon archetypal materials even more than the biblical text.

The shadow king disempowers and curses those outside his realm of worship. If you don't need me, I don't need you. He needs to keep subordinates inferior and in control, whether men or women. They do hold together a certain kind of realm, but it is toxic, dysfunctional and yea-saying. Hitler could hold together other fearful and hateful Germans in his realm; certain popes can hold together card-carrying anti-communists; recent American presidents have been able to see the kingdom of white, rich males. They undoubtedly have real king energy, but it is small and self-serving. They are the Marcoses, Battistas, Samozas and Francos of recent history. They are centered and secure, but in sickness. It is repeated in the wife-beating husband and the embezzling bankers of the savings and loan scandals. All are dark kings, whose only loyalty is to their own company men.

The Warrior

As I mentioned earlier, it is very important that we understand the reality and power of this archetype because it is not going to go away. The warrior is dreamt about in all cultures I know of as the image of courage, persistence, stamina and devotion to a cause. And this image is obviously much needed and very good, but there is a dilemma at the heart of the image.

Essential to the warrior is focus, clarity, absolute allegiance. This image flies in the face of all that we believe about paradox, ambiguity, civility, patience and compromise. If the warrior gives too readily into these, he is by definition no longer in submission to a good king. Without a good king, a warrior is frankly naive, dangerous and probably responsible for most of the aimless and almost recreational violence on this earth. The good warrior doubles his efforts when exhausted, his goal is always beyond the private ego, and he has a sense of necessary and appropriate force to achieve his purposes—no more and no less. He does not need enemies, but neither is he naive about enemies. He is loyal to what deserves loyalty and focuses on the task without preoccupation with his own comfort or security. By any cultural definition that is virtue.

Because we have thrown out the common dark side

of this figure, we have often lost its absolute essential gift. Now unfortunately, we men go to karate classes, the Persian Gulf or fundamentalist churches with this energy because we have not learned how to integrate it with healthy western Christianity. Except for the medieval ideal of the knight of faith, the West has largely missed this archetype. The East understands it better with the martial arts of karate, judo, aikido, the traditions of the noble samurai and the shambala warrior. This probably explains why we have been incapable of accepting the clear nonviolent teaching of Jesus. It's just not in our understanding, even though we had so many saints like Francis and Ignatius who were first of all warriors—and merely transfigured the energy.

The Black Knight/Dark Warrior

Quite simply, the dark warrior is either not in submission to a king or he is in submission to a bad king. He defines what is moral and immoral within himself, by his own egocentric criteria. He normally sees any kind of weakness or femininity as bad because it keeps him from his fanatic focus. I am personally convinced of the essential evil of militarism (on the right or on the left) because they normally have to train and brutalize the young man into simplistic thinking, propaganda and a massive repression of normal human feeling. Fortunately, we have sports and games, albeit a deteriorated but safe way for warriors to act out. Unfortunately, there is no real moral good or virtue to defend.

The Magician

This compelling image is the archetype of awareness, consciousness, growth and transformation. He leads us to see the depth, meaning and especially the shadow side of ourselves and all things. He shows us that things are not what they seem when looked at with "the third eye," which he helps us develop. As such, the magician or court jester is always a threat to the establishment, and it was once his job to keep the king honest and lighthearted. In the lower form the magician is a clown, a trickster or the Native American coyote. In the highest form he is the prophet or truth speaker. But his mantle covers a broad cast of characters: the father confessor, the ritual elder, the shaman, the spirit guide, the sorcerer, the medicine man, the mentor, the spiritual director, the liturgist and, in most cultures, the priest.

It is disappointing to me that priesthood has been made more into the king than the magician in Catholicism. It might account for many of our losses. We even renamed the three magi of Matthew 2 the three kings, even though there is no scriptural evidence for such. The western Church has consistently been more comfortable with kings than wise men. The wise men are always saying to the kings, like Nathan to David, "You are the man!" (2 Samuel 12:7).

The Evil Sorcerer

When a clergyman, a therapist, a guru or a faith-healer starts believing his own press, he is in trouble. When he accepts the awesome projection that people around send toward him as his own, the downward slide begins. If a spiritual leader does not have a strong sense of himself as a humble instrument, if he is not himself in submission to wise spiritual direction, he is perhaps the most dangerous of all the archetypes.

How does one handle the mantle of spiritual power? Frankly, most people don't do it very well. It is too inflating and associates you with the gods. To "traffic in holy things" was once called the egregious sin of simony, and it is always the great temptation of the professionally religious person. I have great sympathy for the major religious figures who have fallen in recent years. If you do not have a strong tradition of spiritual direction (and I mean direction), illusion and infantile grandiosity are almost inevitable in this area. When we wear special clothes, we are asking for this projection. We can use it well to heal, to forgive, to proclaim, to celebrate the holy mysteries. But we can also use it too easily as images and avoid the substance. I always tell the bishops and priests to be careful and aware when they put on those vestments and miters. It's OK, but make sure there is someplace where you can go and take them off—and honest folks can say "bull" to you.

The Lover

When we are captured by the archetype of the lover, we know how to delight, to appreciate, to enjoy that which is good, true and beautiful. We see the color, form, texture and ultimate gratuity of things. In its highest state, therefore, it is the contemplative who can value things in themselves and for themselves and see the hidden beauty of "deep down things." It is also the poet, the artist, the musician, the romantic, those who know how to sip the divine nectar in all events and relationships.

Without the lover, life is frankly boring and eventually sour. If the king holds the real together in unity, the warrior protects the necessary boundaries of the real, the magician shows us how to live the paradox and dark side of the real, then the lover holds it all together with the sweet glue of appreciation and occasional ecstasy. The lover does not apologize for pleasure or joy. He is the fertility god in every man, always ready to dance and display. In mythology he is Dionysius, in literature perhaps Zorba the Greek and in Christianity he is the fiery Holy Spirit who blows where he wills.

Unfortunately the archetype of the lover has always been a bit wild and scary for the rational western Church. He fell into the unconscious, but periodically shows himself in movements like the Renaissance, the worship of the Madonna (fertility was more safely contained and valued in the feminine), elaborate liturgies, saints like Francis of Assisi, Philip Neri and John XXIII, plus the predictable pendulum swings like the hippy generation and the sexual revolution. The lover will not be denied his entrance.

The Addict

When the lover can no longer enjoy, he will create instant and artificial enjoyment. When the lover is not allowed, he goes underground and finds secret and often destructive pleasures. When the lover is rejected, he retreats into negativity, cynicism and self-destruction.

Without the sweetness of the lover, life is frankly not worth living. The usual substitute is to resort to patterns. Patterns of order, patterns of cold duty, patterns of seeming control, patterns of thinking (obsessive), patterns of feeling (hysteric), patterns of hoarding and protecting (paranoid) and patterns of instant gratification like drinking, drugs, buying, promiscuity and overeating. He moves toward narcissism, caring for himself, because he does not feel cared for by life itself.

It is clear that our culture largely falls into this category. We are would-be and wounded lovers. We were somehow given promises here that did not come to pass, and we lack the cultural discipline and containers to hold us back from the long slide downward. Programs for addictions will continue to grow in numbers, in need and in effectiveness. They have named the shape of sin better than the contemporary Churches, who still do not see the connection between their repression of the positive lover archetype and the widespread emergence of the addict. If we had a more positive and integrated attitude toward pleasure, sexuality and embodiment, we would probably not have the destructive overreaction we see today. The rejected god normally returns as a demon.

♦ ♦ ♦

These different faces of the masculine attract us at the different times of our life. There is no correct pattern or superior archetype, in my opinion. The important thing is that we honor all of them and each of them when they show themselves in our friendships and fascinations.

There will normally be one that we are already strongly identified with, and usually one or the other that we mistrust or even deny. He often holds the secret to our wholeness. David, for example, was clearly king, warrior and lover. Until he receives the prophet/magician Nathan, he is still unwhole and even dangerous to himself and others.

The important thing is that we stay on the path and let the four parts of our soul mutually regulate and balance one another. If you overidentify with one for too long, you will normally move toward the dark side. In other words, if you are only a king, unbalanced by warrior, lover and magician, you will soon be a bad king. If you are only a lover, with no sense of king or warrior boundaries, you will soon be an addict. If you are only a warrior, without the nuancing of the magician, you will probably end up a terrorist or a fanatic.

If you fear that this is a new game of "dungeons and dragons," as one super-Christian accused me of, I encourage you to examine the traditional baptismal rite. Right after the holy dunking, the priest anoints you with the cross of the crucified (the lover), and encourages you to follow Christ as priest (magician), prophet (warrior) and king "unto everlasting life." Jesus in his life and in his teaching is easily the "Lord of the Four Quarters."

29

The Grand Father

The father quest seems to be a search for ultimate origin and meaning. This place toward which we are always moving in our spiritual journey is symbolized by the archetype of the grandfather—the grand father.

I myself was blessed with a grand father in the person of my own dad—which is why, perhaps, I identified more with the archetype of the grandfather than the boy even when I was young. My father is a simple man, not highly educated, but very wise. He has the wisdom to know what he knows and to know what he does not know. He also has the wisdom to trust that what he does not understand is good, even if he does not understand it. He has a great respect for the goodness of others. And he can encourage others to trust in their own goodness and to go their own way, even if their way is not his way. Because of his ability to trust and encourage me even when he did not understand where God was calling me, I was able to become a priest and venture into a personal vocation that was very different from my father's.

Even when I was an adolescent, my father grandly

209

trusted and affirmed me. When I wanted to go out, he never demanded that I explain where I was going. He simply trusted me, and through his trust I learned responsibility. Now when I am older, he sometimes comes and listens to a talk that I am giving, and I feel that same trust coming from him. He does not always understand, I'm sure, everything I'm saying, but his lack of comprehension does not diminish his trust in me. I can see him sitting in the front row and I can sense him feeling that whatever I am saying has to be good, just because I'm saying it. His respect for me enables me to be the man that I am and to say what I have to say.

When we can trust others like that—when we can trust God and trust life, even when we do not fully understand—we too can be grand fathers. When we can let go of our need to be perfect and our need to succeed, we can encourage the perfection and the success of others. When we can let go of our fear of failure and our fear of pain, we are free to trust life just as it comes and affirm that, if it comes from God, it must be good. We are free to relinquish the center stage and to stand on the sidelines while we remain in solidarity with those who need our support.

Grand father energy is an energy that is quiet and secure. It has been tested and it has not been found wanting. It does not need to prove itself any longer, and so it can approve the efforts of others who are as yet not sure of themselves. Children can feel secure in the presence of their grandparents because, while mom and dad are still rushing to find their way through life's journey, grandpa and grandma can create a space where the journey has found its end and purpose. Women also radiate grand father energy insofar as they have discovered and integrated the maleness within them. We might call that grand mother energy.

Grand fathers can deeply trust life precisely because they have come to terms with death. They know that pain is not the enemy, but that fear of pain is. They have lived through enough of life to understand that in the long run life is stronger than death. Life has a vitality which may be temporarily slowed down, but inevitably life energy will overcome the destructive forces of death. We see this principle at work on the large scale in the Second and Third Worlds, where despite years of oppression people are insisting on their rights to be free and independent. We see it also at work at lesser levels were groups are working to improve their situations and where individuals overcome great odds, fighting against poverty, addiction and disease, to lead fulfilling and rewarding lives.

Grand fathers recognize the surge of the divine spirit in the human situation. Because they can trust that ultimately God is in control, they can let go of the desire to control reality and to bend others to their will. They can stop trying to force life, as they often did when they were younger men, and simply allow it to flow in the patterns which eventually—if not immediately and directly—lead to greater life.

This is not to say that grand fathers are naive. They have seen enough of death that they know what it looks like, even when it comes under the guise of false promises and clever rationalizations. But they can look beyond the ignorance of the young who desire money and success, power and pleasure, with the wisdom of knowing that in the long run these are transitory illusions. They have heard enough of politicians' promises and advertisers' claims to realize that these are largely empty, but they are not disturbed by the hollowness of talk because they stand on the solidity of life's reality. They know what's worth fighting for and what isn't.

Younger men need to fight against the forces of death in their own lives and in the life of their society—and rightly so, for their calling is to assume responsibility for the direction of life and to courageously work for their own good and the good of others. Grand fathers, however, understand that every human decision inevitably mixes good and bad, and that every social situation is a mixture of light and darkness. The courage of the grand father, therefore, is not to fight death but to affirm life in the face of death. They recognize that, as Jesus said, "No one is good but God alone" (Mark 10:18b), so they are free of the illusion that any other good is completely good or that any particular need is absolutely necessary.

In fact, the first half of life is as necessary as the second. To presumptuously jump to stage two before fighting, needing, "cursing" and failing is often a lazy and dishonest surrender. I worry about young men who have no heroic desires, no egocentric passion, no wanderlust and no "sin." They are in danger of never becoming grand fathers.

Grand fathers can trust life because they have seen more of it than younger men have, and they can trust death because they are closer to it than younger men are. Something has told them along the way who they are now is not the final stage of their being. Just as you cannot be a biological grandfather when you are only in your twenties, you cannot be a spiritual grand father when you are very young. You need to be close enough to your own death to see it coming and recognize it for what it is, while realizing that it is not the end of life. Death is what it is. Death is not good, but it is a part of life, and life is good. The body is a lesson; once we have learned the lesson, we can let go of it.

The soul of the grand father is large enough to embrace the death of the ego and to affirm the life of God in itself and others, despite the inevitability of physical death. Its spaciousness accepts all the opposites in life—masculine and feminine, unity and difference, victory and defeat, us and them, and so on—because it has accepted the opposition of death itself. To the grand father, death is no longer an enemy, but as St. Francis called it, a "welcome sister."

The grand father no longer needs the luxury of utterly clear principles to assure him of each decision. If he has walked the hero's journey, he knows that his beliefs have less to do with unarguable conclusions than sometimes scary encounters with life and the living God. He has come to realize that spiritual growth is not so much learning, as it is unlearning, a radical openness to the truth no matter what the consequences or where it leads. He understands that he does not so much grasp the truth as let go of the personal obstacles to truth. He is aware that people do not really understand if they too strongly approve or disapprove of something, for there is too much ego blocking their vision. He has learned that conversion is a process of listening ever more deeply to the other—and to the Other.

Perhaps more than anything else, one becomes a grand father in learning to deal with limits graciously. Which, of course, is learned by facing concrete and offensive limitations. In that sense a young man can take on significant grand father strength, as we sometimes see in the youthful bodies of the handicapped or the oppressed. The joyful acceptance of a limited world, of which I am only a small moment and part, is probably the clearest indication of mature male energy. What he once fought for—perfect freedom—he now finds in the even imperfect events and institutions of this world. Witness a St. Paul or a Nelson Mandela in prison. The grand father largely mistrusts the world's definition of freedom. Like Aristotle, he understands that freedom only works in a person or group committed to virtue.

Reflections such as these make me wonder if there is much chance of achieving true human freedom in this world. Few heads of state seem to have much inner depth, young men are told to accept the system and succeed in it and forty-eight percent of American men are now employed by the government or the top ten giant corporations. In such a culture, who is willing to pay the price of true freedom? Who can even recognize it?

No civilization has ever survived unless the elders have been willing to pass on their acquired wisdom to the youth. Yet we no longer have any strong expectation or expressed need for this to happen. Even Catholic colleges have largely become places of job preparation rather than intellectual and spiritual development. And in many churches the great Abrahamic journey has been dropped in favor of catechism answers and fundamentalist short-circuiting. Wisdom does not die unless it has been allowed to die. Most people are still alive enough to recognize wisdom if it is offered.

Which returns us to the addictive system we talked about in the beginning of this book. I think we are going to have to admit that we have idolatrously worshiped our system, especially after the somewhat false euphoria of World War II. America became our salvation, not the gospel. To quote the grand father, T. S. Eliot:

> "Here were decent godless people:
> Their only monument the asphalt road
> And a thousand lost golf balls."[28]

The only choice we were offered was between a so-called conservative interpretation of this idolatry, which was supposed to respect law and tradition, and the tried and true. These false grandfathers ended up loving security more than truth, a proper self-image more than any semblance of faith journey. And the so-called liberals are usually anything but "free," as their only description of freedom is a sort of naive "everybody and everything is good," terrified by the masculine "No!" and finally incapable of meaningful boundaries and real identity. Their tolerance is not the wise understanding of the grand father but the feel-good tolerance of the little boy who does not yet know who he is.

There is something both territorial and spacious about the grand father. He knows his boundaries and he

---

[28]Eliot, T.S. "Choruses from the Rock," *Complete Poems and Plays, 1909-1950*. New York, N.Y.: Harcourt Brace Jovanovich, Inc., 1971, p. 103.

knows his center, but he does not need to overprotect either of them. They just are. He can describe and share them with interested friends or young people, but he does not need to force their journey to be just like his in order to feel confirmed. The spiritually mature man always has a sense of his ground, and he is not afraid to defend his turf if the center is threatened. But he knows that the boundaries themselves are mere accidentals in most cases. With the calm security of Jesus, the grand father can speak to the young zealots: "Do not prevent him.... For whoever is not against us is for us" (Mark 9:39-40). And yet with the same security he can justify and defend his territory in relation to clear evil: "Whoever is not with me is against me, and whoever does not gather with me scatters" (Matthew 12:30). Real wisdom is the ability to know when each command is appropriate. There is a time for each.

The chaos and pluralism of our times will probably continue to push many men toward taking refuge behind false boundaries, such as patriarchy, nationalism, racism, fundamentalism and sexism, instead of remaining on the labyrinthine journey called faith. Others will continue to move toward psycho-babble and New Age shapelessness precisely in order to avoid all boundaries and surrenders. I cannot imagine a true grand father who is not a contemplative in some form. And a contemplative is one who lives and returns to the center within himself and yet knows that the Center is not himself. He is only a part, but a gracious and grateful part at that.

Maybe we need to stop describing this in terms of concepts and just name a few grand fathers whom we all might know. We need their power in our times, and only their lives and witness can give it to us. I know you could add many more, and I hope you do, but these are some who occur to me: Abraham Lincoln, Albert Schweitzer, Dag Hammarsköld, U Thant, John XXIII, Dietrich Bonhoeffer, Mikhail Gorbachev, Jean Vanier, Thich Nhat Hanh, Martin Luther King, Jr., Mohandas Gandhi, Nelson Mandela, Anwar Sadat, Abraham Heschel, Thomas Merton, Dom Helder Camara, Thomas Dooley, Hubert Humphrey, John Howard Griffin, Julius Nyrere.

Needless to say, we are not mass-producing elders in American society today, for it takes a wild man to call forth a wild man. It sometimes feels to me as though we are waiting for a global act of spiritual spontaneous combustion. But we can all go to the Source for the fire—the source within and the Source whom we call God.

Afterword

Masculine spirituality. Perhaps the term sounds new, different, even wrong or unnecessary. Why would we bother speaking of a spirituality that is especially masculine or male? Is there anything to be learned here? Anything that can help both men and women to meet the Christ? I am convinced that there is. Let's see if we can summarize it.

First, I want to say that a masculine spirituality is not just for men, although it is men who are most likely going to have to rediscover and exemplify it. Strangely, it is an approach that many women are more in touch with today than men. Women have been encouraged and even forced to work on their inner lives more than men in our culture.

In general, they are far ahead of men in integrating the masculine and feminine parts of themselves. Their inner journeys have left many of us men in the dust. Our sisters' pursuit of the authentic feminine has made the brothers aware that there is also an authentic masculine. But what is it?

Quite simply it is the other side of the feminine

energy. It is the other pole, the contrary, the balance.

In the Chinese view of the universe, it is the yang, or active masculine principle, that is always the necessary complement to yin, the passive feminine principle. For the Judeo-Christian tradition, it is half of the image of God: "God created man in his image... male and female he created them" (Genesis 1:27).

I am not saying that males are characterized by exclusively masculine energy and women hold only feminine, quite the contrary, although there has been a tendency in most cultures to stereotype, classify and hold the sexes in one predictable type of energy and behavior. Unfortunately, I believe, this tendency has kept us immature, unwhole, compulsive and unready for living a life of true love—human or divine.

St. Paul says, "...there is not male and female; for you are all one in Christ Jesus" (Galatians 3:28). The new humanity that we are pointed toward is not neuter or unisex or oversexed, all of which make love impossible. In Christ we are whole, one, in union, integrated, wholly holy. That is the final product of the Spirit making all things one. It is the consummate achievement of God in Christ who reconciles all things within himself (Colossians 1:20) and invites us into the ongoing reconciliation of all things (Ephesians 5:20).

As a celibate male religious, I can make little sense of my state unless I find some way to awaken and love my own inner feminine soul. Without it, I am merely a self-centered bachelor, a would-be creator, a dried-up root. A man without his feminine soul is easily described. His personality will move toward the outer superficial world and his head will be his control tower. He will build, explain, use, fix, manipulate, legislate, order and play with whatever he bothers to touch, but he will not really touch it at all. For he does not know the inside of things.

In fact, he is afraid of it, and that is why the control tower of reason and pseudocontrol works overtime. It is the only way he can give himself a sense of security and significance. He is trapped in part of the picture, which is dangerous precisely because he thinks it is the whole picture. He is trapped inside the false masculine. Corporately, this has become the myth of western civilization. It is largely written by men who have controlled the power, the money, the corporations, the Church, the military, the morality books. What we call reality, and are almost totally addicted to, is largely a construct of men who have frankly never worked on their inner lives. They have not gone inside, they have not learned trust, vulnerability, prayer or poetry. They, and the civilization we have inherited from them, are in great part unwhole or even sick.

Until males and cooperating females recognize this unwholeness, this anti-Christianity posing as reality, we have no hope of loving the full Christ. We will, in fact, be threatened by this unwholeness and replace (as we generally have) a daring religious faith with little schemes of salvation. Basically, this is a transfer of the business world of win/achieve/prove/success/control to the realm of the Spirit. And it just doesn't work. God knows, we have tried for enough centuries! There must be a better way. And there is. It's called conversion.

Conversion to what? Conversion to what we might call the not-me. By that I mean conversion to the other, the alien, the would-be enemy. In other words, men must be converted to the feminine, women to the masculine. Maybe that is why God made sexual attraction so compelling. If we are converted to this non-self, everything changes.

Having undergone this conversion, we are whole, centered. From this position we can see through eyes other than our half-blinded ones. We see the other side of things. We see that the enemy is not enemy but spiritual helpmate. There is nothing more to defend and nothing more to be afraid of once we have met and accepted our inner opposite.

A masculine spirituality would emphasize action over theory, service to the human community over religious discussions, speaking the truth over social graces and doing justice over looking nice. Without a complementary masculine, spirituality becomes overly feminine (which is really a false feminine!) and is characterized by too much inwardness, preoccupation with relationships, a morass of unclarified feeling and endless self-protectiveness.

In my humble masculine opinion I believe much of the modern, sophisticated Church is swirling in the false feminine. It is one of the main reasons that doers, movers, shakers and change agents have largely given up on Church people and Church groups. As one very effective woman said to me, "After a while you get tired of the in-house jargon that seems to go nowhere." A false feminine spirituality is the trap of those with lots of leisure, luxury and liberal ideas. They have the option not to do. Their very liberalism becomes an inoculation against the whole and radical gospel.

A masculine spirituality would be one that encourages men to take the radical gospel journey from their unique beginning point, in their own unique style, with their own unique goals—without doubt or apology or imitation of their sisters (or mothers, for that matter). That takes immense courage and self-possession. Such a man has life for others and knows it. He does not need to push, intimidate or play the power games common to other men because he possesses his power with surety and calm self-confidence. He is not opinionated or arrogant, but he knows. He is not needy or bothered by status symbols because he is. He does not need monogrammed briefcases and underwear, his identity is settled and secure—and within. He possesses his soul and does not give it lightly to corporations, armies, nation-states or the acceptable collective thinking.

Saints are people who are whole. They trust their masculine soul because they have met the Father. He taught them about anger, passion, power and clarity. He told them to go all the way through and pay the price for it. He shared with them his own creative seed, his own decisive word, his own illuminating Spirit. They are comfortable knowing and they are comfortable not knowing. They can care and not care without guilt. They can act without success because they have named their fear of failure. They do not need to affirm or deny, judge or ignore. But they are free to do all of them with impunity. The saints are invincible. They are men!

There are many reasons, I'm sure, why a healthy masculine spirituality has taken so long to emerge. The state needed conformists and unfeeling warriors to go about its business, and "holy Mother Church" seemed to want children more than bridegrooms. But I am convinced there is a more fundamental reason why men and women have failed to love and trust their masculine energy. It is this: The vast majority of people in western civilization suffer from what I identified earlier in the book as a father wound. Those who have this father wound have never been touched by their human father. Either he had no time, no freedom or no need, but the result is children who have no masculine energy. They will lack self-confidence and the ability to do, to carry through, to trust themselves—because they were never trusted by him.

If there is one very good reason for God to reveal himself as the Father of Jesus, it is because that is where most people are unfeeling, unbelieving and unwhole. With Philip the Apostle, we all join in, "Master, show us the Father, and that will be enough for us" (John 14:8). Without facing, feeling and restoring this wound, I am sure that most people will continue to live lives of pseudomasculinity: business and bravado as usual, dishonest power instead of honest powerlessness. And the sons and daughters of the next generation will repeat the sad process—unfathered.

Is there a way out? There is. But only for "men"— that is, for people, both men and women—who will act. There is no way to masculinity. Masculinity is the way. So, name the wound. Feel and weep over the wound. That is strength, not weakness. Seek the face of the Father. That is action and journey, not passivity. Own and take full responsibility for your life and behavior. Don't blame, sit in shame or wait for warm feelings or miracles. Act as if. Do it. Go with it. Risk it.

Call it phallic faith, if you will, but masculine spirituality does not doubt the seed within. Today, God's sons are without dignity, self-confidence, true power. We look like the oppressors, dear sisters, but have no doubt we are really the oppressed. We believed the false promises of the system even more than you and now we are trapped at what is supposed to be the top. We need you, we need our feminine souls, we need fathers and brothers, we need an also-masculine-God to find our way back into the human circle. We need ourselves—from the inside. And we need to act—on the outside.

The spiritual man in mythology, in literature and in the great world religions has an *excess of life*, he *knows* he has it, makes no apology for it and finally recognizes that he does not need to protect it. It is for others.